A CONCISE HISTORY OF

AZERBAIJAN

Azerbaijan's History from the Medieval Turkic
Dynasties to the First Turkic Republic

Jahangir Zeynaloglu

Riverbed Publishers, All Rights Reserved

Copyright © 1997, 2020 Translated by F. Abasov, Riverbed Publishers, All Rights Reserved

No part of this book may be reproduced, or stored in a retrieval system, or transmitted in any form or by any means, electronic, mechanical, photocopying, recording, or otherwise, without express written permission of the publisher.

A Concise History of Azerbaijan

This brief but informative book is one of the first works by the 20th century Azerbaijani historians. The author describes the rich and turbulent history of Azerbaijan covering essentially all major periods of the Azerbaijani history: ancient times, various Azerbaijani Turkic dynasties in the Middle Ages, Independent Khanates and the events preceding the establishment of the Azerbaijani Democratic Republic, the first Turkic and Muslim republic in history. The book contains interesting facts for the general reader as well as experts on Azerbaijan.

Photos and Illustrations:

Front Cover: The Mardakan Fortress near Baku, Azerbaijan

Part 1 – The Church of Kish, a Caucasian Albanian church in Azerbaijan

Part 2 – Ganja during the Independent Atabeg State

Part 4 – Qara Yusif, a Qaraqoyunlu ruler, charging on a battlefield

Part 6 – The Battle of Ganja 1826

Dear reader,

A Concise History of Azerbaijan is a unique history book written by Mr. Jahangir Zeynaloglu (1892-1944) before Soviet Russia occupied the Azerbaijan Democratic Republic in April 1920. This work reflects the position of an Azerbaijani historian during the independent Azerbaijani Democratic Republic of 1918-1920.

As the author himself explains he could not have the book published in Azerbaijan since the country was already under the Russian Bolshevik rule in 1923. Hence, the book was originally published in Ottoman Turkish in Istanbul. A notable feature of the translation is the conversion of the Islamic calendar into the Julian calendar using a special formula, which could lead to some differences in certain dates.

The translator has not made any attempt to verify or correct any of the information in this book in an effort to keep the original text intact. In certain instances, we provide notes to clarify various points made by the author. All illustrations, photos, chronology of events and maps have been added by the publisher.

Mr. Zeynaloglu's book does not cover the period after 1920. The Russian 11th Red Army occupied Baku on April 28, 1920. Northern Azerbaijan lived under the Soviet rule for 71 years until 1991, when the Azerbaijani Parliament declared the independence of the country again. The book does not include the history of Southern Azerbaijan which roughly comprises East and West Azerbaijan, Zanjan provinces in Iran starting from the 16th century.

Jahangir Zeynal Bey Oglu Nesibov was born in Shusha, Azerbaijan in 1892. He served as an officer in the National Army of the Azerbaijan Democratic Republic. He emigrated to Turkey after the Soviet forces occupied Azerbaijan in 1920. He published three other books while in Turkey: The Land of the Shirvanshahs, The Khanate Period of Our History and The Azerbaijani Folk Wisdoms (Simple Folks Say It As It Is). In 1931, the author presented the first copy of the Land of the Shirvanshahs to Mustafa Kemal Ataturk, the founder of the modern Turkish Republic, who gratefully accepted it.

From the Publisher

A CONCISE HISTORY OF AZERBAIJAN

This book is dedicated to the blessed souls of the Azerbaijani and Anatolian Turks who gave their lives for the freedom of Azerbaijan.

Jahangir Zeynaloglu

A CONCISE HISTORY OF AZERBAIJAN

CONTENTS

Prologue	6
Part One, Pre-Independence Period	7
Part Two, The Independent Atabeg State	23
Part Three, The Mongols (Ilkhanids, Chobanids, Jelairids)	32
Part Four, The Independent Qaraqoyunlu and Aghqoyunlu States	48
Part Five, The Era of the Independent Khanates	65
Part Six, The Russian Occupation of Azerbaijan	94
Part Seven, The Period of the Independent Republic	115
The Bibliography	126
The Chronology of Key Events	127

"Your noble souls are blessed forever

Your sacred memories we always revere."

Memmed Emin Resulzade
One of the Founders of the Azerbaijan Democratic Republic

Prologue

A new Turkic state has emerged in the East. Although the Azerbaijan Democratic Republic was founded and its independence declared in 1918, this country was not as successful in getting aid from the international community as its neighbors. One of the neighboring countries, Armenia, received assistance from the USA, while Georgia, another neighbor, was recognized by the Bern Conference.

Unfortunate Azerbaijan despite its glorious past and vast natural resources remains unknown to the world even today. Not only do not foreign countries know much about Azerbaijan, but its closest Muslim neighbors are also completely unaware of its history and present situation. One cannot even find a single serious literary work written on the subject.

Therefore, it is our sacred national duty to study our history and be prepared for the challenges of independence.

We, the Azerbaijani Turks, have no aggressive plans against any nation. We just strive to protect the independence and national dignity of our beautiful motherland. This is our sole objective.

This is the reason we, the Azerbaijanis, should do all in our power to join European organizations quickly in order to study and introduce European democratic ideals and values in our society. Otherwise, our independence will be lost, and our ancient nation will be doomed. This objective should be comprehended by every Turk. In a nutshell, we must know ourselves and make sure others know our culture and history. It was precisely these ideals that compelled me to write this book.

I beg your forgiveness for my shortcomings, and I hope that they will be forgiven for my intentions are noble.

I originally wrote this concise history book in Azerbaijani Turkish. However, the ongoing turmoil in Azerbaijan did not allow me to publish it in our motherland. Finally, here in Istanbul, I adapted its language to the local dialect so that the book could be understood in both Turkey and Azerbaijan.

May God help me in this endeavor!

Jahangir Zeynaloglu, Istanbul, Turkey, 1923

PART ONE

Pre-Independence Period

Ancient History

Azerbaijan has witnessed endless wars and natural disasters throughout its history. Consequently, most of the history works, folk tales, historical data, and other information relating to our ancient history have been destroyed. Very little has been recorded. Initially, I intended to describe the events after the first independent Azerbaijani government omitting the pre-Islamic history altogether. However, I later reconsidered my position and deemed it useful to give some insight into the ancient period of our history.

Midia, Aghvan, Albania

Many centuries ago, the southern part of Azerbaijan was called Midia, roughly covering the territory south of the river of Arax. The northern part came to be known as Aghvan-Arran, and the area known today as Shirvan was called Albania[1] (*more commonly known as Caucasian Albania*).

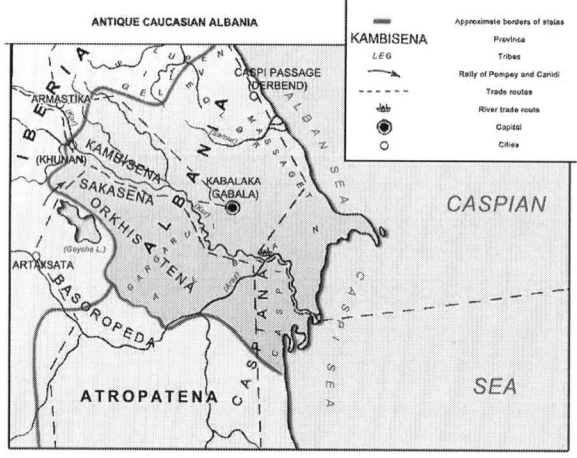

The Map of Ancient Azerbaijan including Caucasian Albania and Atropatena

---

[1] Aghvan (Aghuvan) means the country of fire worshipping (Zoroastrians). "Ahu" means fire in most languages. In Chinese "aghi" means a glowing mountain; in Russian fire is "ogon"; the Latin "agnis" stands for fire etc. The Arabs transformed Aghvan into Mughan which in Arabic means fireworshipper (mugh-mughan). Arran or Aran is its Turkish version. Nowadays the pasturable and arid lands in Azerbaijan are called Aran. Albania means a mountainous country in Greek. The Arnauds who live in the Balkans and have no relation to the Azerbaijanis in the Caucasus were also named Albanians by the Greeks because of the mountainous terrain.

The Situation in Arran and Aghvan

The country enjoyed very fertile lands. But its most fertile lands on the coastal areas were not utilized to their full extent as they were often flooded by the rising level of the Caspian Sea. According to a legend, the population consisted of twenty-six tribes that spoke different languages and constantly warred with each other. The sun and the moon were the principal idols of their pagan religion.

The largest houses of God of the Aghvanis were located in the cities of Gabala and Samukh (*in the north of the present-day Republic of Azerbaijan, the publisher's note*). These people were notorious in having the utmost respect for the elderly. Their dead were buried together with their clothes and other belongings.

The famous Greek geographer Strabo wrote that there were twenty six languages used in this country. However, the Arabs claimed that there was a much larger number of tribes and almost three hundred languages were spoken in the entire Caucasus. The Arabs called the Caucasus the mountain of languages.

Arran was in the state of permanent warfare with its neighbors. The province of Sisagan[2] (*modern-day Karabakh region of Azerbaijan Republic)* and the city of Ganja were changing hands all the time. Finally, the borders of Arran were extended, and its capital was moved from Barda to Ganja.

Since Tabriz (*a city in northwestern Azerbaijan province of modern Iran*) used to be called Ganja at that time too, modern Ganja was called Ganja of Aghvan. After the Arab occupation of Iran in the 7th century, the residents of Arran resisted invading Arab armies.

The Kura river played a vital role in the development of this country since the river served as the main transport artery of Arran. Both fire-worshippers coming to visit their sacred sites and merchants from India on trade trips traveled via the Kura.

---

[2] Modern Qarabagh (Karabakh) was called "Sisagan" by foreigners and "Siyunya" by the Armenians. Later the Seljuks named it Karabakh, meaning "a black garden" in Azerbaijani Turkish.

Ancient Cities

The city of Barda was one of the major trade partners of India since it was located on the navigable river Kura. Barda was a very prosperous and wealthy capital due to its enormous fish resources, fertile lands, plenty of cattle, and precious stones. Today it is the capital of one of the Azerbaijani provinces.

The word "Barda" comes from the ancient Greek with "bar" meaning a nipple and "de" signifying a city or town. It meant the city of nipples. The famous Russian historian Shopen wrote that there were two tribes in the southern Caucasus one of which worshipped female genitals while the other held female breast sacred. He also contended that Barda was built by the latter tribe. Georgians, however, claim that a famous Georgian athlete by the name of Bardus founded this city. The Georgians back this theory with numerous legends.

Ganja. Genj meant a "coffer" or "treasure" in Persian. Ganja is said to have been named so for its enormous wealth. After the relocation of the capital from Barda to Ganja, the latter became to be known as Ganja of Aghvan. Today it is the center of the Ganja province in Azerbaijan and the second largest city in the country.

Beyleqan. It used to be a large city south of Barda. Today we can see only the ruins of that great city. The city was full of wooden pagan idols. That is why Beyleqan was called a "tree center" from Greek. Later the Arabs transformed it into Beyleqan. Hamdullah Mustovfi said that Beyleqan was founded by the Sasanid ruler Qubad ibn Firuz. But it is believed that the city was built much earlier than Qubad's time but was restored and revamped by him.

Sheki. Both the province and its center are called Nukha. Sheki, Sevari and Nukha or Nugha mean the land of women. Amazon women are believed to have ruled this city.

Shirvan. Shirvan is the name of a new province, and its center is the city of Shemakha. Shir is a lion; van means a location or place. Shirvan stands for the country of lions. Shemakha means Sarmag, that is the center of fire worshippers. Nowadays Shemakha is the administrative center of one of the Azerbaijani provinces.

Terter. It is located near Barda. This city that used to play a prominent role in the country's life is now reduced to the size of a small town. In ancient Greek "tur" means a country and "tar" is a woman. So, the city derives its name from Greek meaning the land of women. Historians speculate that Terter was founded by the same tribe that built Barda.

Shamkir. Shams - sun, kir - worshipper. It means the land of sun worshippers. Shamkir is a small town 32 kilometers from Ganja.

Maragha, Irevan (*today's Yerevan, the capital city of the Republic of Armenia*), Tabriz, Nakhichevan and other Azerbaijani cities are believed to have been built by Arab and Turkic rulers after the advent of Islam (*Most of these cities date back to the pre-Islamic period but gained prominence under the Islamic Turkic rulers*).

The Etymology of the name Azerbaijan

The Arab historian Al ibn Al Fegihet Al Hemedani claims that the name Azerbaijan derives from the word Azerbaz ibn Al Iran ibn As Sud ibn AsSam ibn An Nuh. According to Hemedani's theory, our country was named after one of the children of Noah whose name was Azerbaz. The Romans and Byzantines called our country Atropatena which meant the land of fire in ancient Persian. At that time, our motherland was a Mecca for all the fire worshippers of the world. One can still encounter the last Zoroastrian temple near Baku.

The History by Teberi, an Arab historian, states that in the Pahlavi language "azer" stood for a "fire". The pilgrims named the country Azerbaijan since the largest holy fire was in this country.

At a Zoroastrian Temple known as Ateshgah twenty-two kilometers to the east of Baku

This holy temple called Ateshgah was constructed in ancient times. Only in the nineteenth century was it renovated and fixed by an Indian benefactor. Some parts of the temple are believed to have been erected in the 18th century. But it is not clear who originally built it and when. It was especially popular with the Indians. After 1869 the flow of pilgrims shrank dramatically, and the temple's idols and other ornaments were stolen or lost. Nevertheless, the temple's fires are still burning even today. In recent years, the Russian engineer Semyonov studied the gas pipelines that fueled the flames of Ateshgah and used its design to build pipelines to transport natural oil and gas to refineries.

Below is an account from Nasireddin Shah Qajar[3] who was one of the recent people who saw a pilgrim at the temple: "A Hindu was praying in the temple. He was dressed in a white robe and held a small drum in his right hand. Facing east the Hindu would genuflect three times and play his drum. After a few minutes, he finished his prayer and played on a larger drum that was hanging in the center of the temple. When I asked him about the meaning of this drumbeating the Hindu replied that it was to ward off demons. Then he offered me a plate full of food." From Nasireddin Shah's Sefername, 1872.

The Historic Lands of Azerbaijan

Al Hemedani indicated the following boundaries of Azerbaijan in his book Kitab ul-Buldanll: "Azerbaijan's territory stretched from Barda to Zanjan. The cities of Berker, Selmas, Mughan, Khoy, Vergan, Beylegan, Maragha, Neriz and Tabriz were located on these lands. From east to west one could visit the provinces of Deylem, Tarem, and Jilan. The area included such cities as Barda, Saburkhas, Kherenj, Miyanj, Merend, Khoy, Gulsere and Berzend."

Berzend was destroyed but later rebuilt by the Turkic general Mshin. The same book says that Ganja, Jabrvan, Rumiyye and Ashiz also belonged to Azerbaijan. According to this source there was a very important Zoroastrian temple in Ashiz called Azerjeshnis.

Ashiz must be a village today known as Surakhani near Baku. I dare think so because the famous Arab traveler Al Yagubi mentioned this place in his notes as Ashiz or Assir or Safarkhan (Surakhani).

Map of the Modern Republic of Azerbaijan

---

[3] An Iranian Shah of the Azerbaijani Qajar Dynasty from Tabriz (1831-96) (The publisher's note)

The History by Teberi states: "A territory that stretched from Hamadan and Zanjan to Derbend[4] was called Azerbaijan". Hamdullah Mustovfi described Azerbaijan's boundaries as " the lands that covered 95 ferseng (one ferseng is approximately seven kilometers) from Badi-kube to Khalkhal". The renowned book "Mirat ul buldani Nasiri" noted: "The farthest western point of Azerbaijan was Barda and the southernmost point was Zanjan. Deylem and Terem were connecting points."

Other Arab and foreign historians define the Azerbaijani borders very similarly. Obviously, the provinces that comprise the present-day Caucasian Azerbaijan were part of greater Azerbaijan together with Iranian Azerbaijan. Only recently has Azerbaijan been divided into Caucasian and Iranian parts by aggressive imperialist states.

The Early Turkic Settlements in Azerbaijan

The territory of present-day Azerbaijan was home to the Midians from the time immemorial. It is still not clear where the Midians originated from. Only recently has it been confirmed that the Midians were of Turanian (Turkic) descent.

1181 years before Mohammed's Hajj, a tribe known as the Massagets led by their ruler Tomris Khan fought and defeated the Iranian Shah Keykhosrov, an ethnic Persian. Massaget means a white Hun Turk. The ancient Huns had settled in Midia and on the Caspian coast long before those events. The Huns were called by different names such as the Massaget, Abtlit, Alan, Khazar, Hergan, Turkman, etc. Thus, the White Huns settled in Azerbaijan centuries ago and formed the core of the indigenous people.

Before those events, the Eastern or Chinese Turks[5] were shipping their silk to the Midian Turks via the Soghdiye Turks. The Midian Turks in their turn were selling silk to Byzantium. Therefore, the Midian Turks played a crucial role in the commerce between the Chinese and Byzantine empires. The growing trade links were the reason that Chinese and Turan Kings (Mughan Khan) dispatched a special trade envoy by the name of Manyakh to the court of the Iranian Shah Nushirevan Khosrovi in 567.

---

[4] Derbend is located in the Autonomous Republic of Daghestan, Russian Federation (The publisher's note)
[5] Known as the Uighur Turks today (The publisher's note)

Clearly, the Midian Turks who were instrumental in procuring the trade between China and Byzantium had arrived and settled in Midia a few centuries earlier.

Two centuries later during the Arab Islamic Conquest of Azerbaijan, the Arab Abbasid dynasty could not suppress an uprising led by Babek from the Khuremiyye tribe in Azerbaijan and had to invite Turks from Turkestan (Central Asia). The Turkestanis under the command of generals Afshin and Bugha marched to Azerbaijan through Iran and occupied Tiflis and Shirvan in order to cut off Babek's forces from Byzantium and the Khazars. After that Afshin laid siege to the city of Khurram and captured Babek. Babek was later executed. Violent events followed the capture and execution of Babek. Zoroastrian temples were destroyed, and their fires extinguished. The population was either expelled or forced to convert to Islam. These new Turks that included the tribes of Guz (*more commonly known as Oghuz, the publisher's note*), Seljuk, Turkman, Qazakh, Javanshir, Jebrayil, Kengerli and others settled in Azerbaijan. Today some cities and towns are named after those tribes. In our age, there are only a few non-Turks left in the country. Those are fifty thousand Talishs in Lenkoran and about one hundred thousand Tats[6][7] in Ganja, Baku and Quba. The rest of the indigenous population is entirely Turkic.

Babek's statue in Babek City, Nakhichevan, Azerbaijan Republic

Consequently, although some Turks settled in Azerbaijan during the rebellion of Babek in 806-835 most of them as we have explained above had settled here long before the 9th century.

---

[6] Most of the Tats in Azerbaijan today profess Judaism and are also known as the Mountain Jews. Outside of Azerbaijan, large Tat or Mountain Jewish diasporas are located in the US and Israel. (*The publisher's note*)

[7] The Tats are believed to have migrated to Azerbaijan from India and Turkestan. The Tats found in Turkestan today are supposed to be the ancient relatives of the migrants to Azerbaijan.

The Azerbaijani Turks

Certain Turkic tribes such as the Khazars, Seljuks, Moguls, Turkmens, etc. who ruled Azerbaijan at different times settled in the country along with the Huns.

In the course of history, these tribes acclimatized to our nature, found a common language with each other and united. As it is the case everywhere the minorities such as ancient Tats, Talishs, Lezgins and newly arrived Arabs and Kurds melted with the Turkic majority to form a new nation, that is the Azerbaijani Turks. The language of the Azerbaijanis is remarkably simple and on the Turkic language scale is between the Chagatai[8] and Ottoman dialects.

Due to the natural beauty and simplicity of the Azerbaijani Turkish language, it became a Lingua Franca in the Caucasus, southern Russia, parts of Iran, and the rest of Central Asia. Azerbaijanis are Muslim by religion.

The Arab Invasions (643-1052)
The General Political Situation in the Caucasus before and during the Arab Military Campaigns

When Arab armies invaded the Caucasus, its northern part was ruled by the powerful Khazars[9]. The Khazars also controlled the small nations of Ossetians and Alans. Since Armenia was divided between Iran and Byzantium in 428 there was no independent Armenian state when the Arab armies arrived in the region.

Azerbaijan sandwiched between the Khazars and Iran became a battleground for those two states. Various parts of Azerbaijan were repeatedly looted and local people were massacred by these raiders.

Georgia was also a scene of bloody wars between the regional powers. However, due to its geographical location, Georgia managed to retain some degree of autonomy. Istepanoz the Second was the king in Georgia while Iran was ruled by the Sasanids, and Byzantium was under Emperor Iraklis.

---

[8] The Chagatay language was an ancient Turkic language which was the forefather of other Turkic languages in Central Asia such as Uzbek and Uighur (*The publisher's note*)

[9] The Arabs called the Turkic tribe of Bulgars the Khazars. The Bulgars controlled vast territories between Don and Itil (Volga) rivers. The Caspian Sea was also named the Khazar Sea (*it is Khazar Denizi in Turkic languages, the publisher's note*) after the tribe. Khazar means "a bug shell" in Arabic. These Turks were called so because of their unusually narrow eyes. The Russians also called these Turks the Khazars. (*There are other modern linguistic theories regarding the origin of the word Khazar, The publisher's note*).

The Arabs marched towards the Caucasus at this time and engaged in a battle with Byzantium near the river Irmuk. The Byzantines were routed and forced to retreat to the west. Byzantium never recovered from that defeat. The Arabs defeated the Iranians in Gadsiya in 636 and in the year 637 they took the city of Tabriz. In 638, the Arab armies crossed the river Arax into the northern part of Azerbaijan.

The First Arab Incursion

In 643, Caliph Omar ibn Khattab ordered three armies into Azerbaijan. One was headed by Bekr ibn Abdullah. The Azerbaijani ruler Isfendiyar fought Bekr's armies but soon was defeated and taken prisoner. Isfendiyar was brought to the army headquarters but was not beheaded. Bekr spared his life and kept him in his inner circle as Isfendiyar knew the Azerbaijani terrain, customs, and traditions very well. Isfendiyar together with his servicemen converted to Islam.

Meanwhile, two other Arab armies one led by Ismet ibn Ferged and the other by Semek ibn Kherrashe entered Azerbaijan. All three armies were put under the central command and soon occupied most of Azerbaijan. Later Behram ibn Farrokhzad, one of the local warlords, drafted an army and waged ruthless wars against the Arabs, but his forces were eventually defeated and had to retreat. All of Azerbaijan with the only exception of Derbend came under Arab control. Most of the population eventually converted to Islam.

Bekr ibn Abdullah sent precious gifts to the Caliph as a tribute and asked him for further instructions stressing the threat from the Khazars in the north. At the order of the Caliph, Bekr left Ismet ibn Ferged in charge of Azerbaijan and marched against Derbend[10]. However, the Caliph believed that the army marching towards Derbend was not large enough to take the city. He promptly ordered two more armies to mobilize for Derbend: one from Basra under general Sirag ibn Omer and the other from Jezire headed by Habib ibn Muslime. They joined Bekr's forces and launched an offensive on Derbend. Shehrizad, the ruler of Derbend, refused to shed the blood of the city's innocent residents in the face of the overwhelming Arab troops and sent an envoy to Bekr's camp to sign a peace treaty. Shehrizad also expounded the importance of Derbend for the security of Azerbaijan. He complained about the Rus, Khazar and Alans

---

[10] In the pre-Islamic era, a number of fortresses were erected in order to protect Azerbaijan from the Khazar raids. The largest fortress is that of Derbend which survives to our day. Azerbaijani Turks called it "Demir Gapi" or Iron Gates, and the Arabs preferred the name of "Bab ul Abvab" that is " The Gate of Gates".

in the North and offered to defend the northern gates to Azerbaijan in return for a small tax on his fiefdom. The Caliph was immediately informed of this proposal. He ordered Bekr to conclude similar treaties with all the neighboring governments. Sirag ibn Omer died in Derbend. Following his will, a general by the name of Abdul Rehman was appointed the commander of the army. He attacked the Khazars together with Shehrizad, and later also died in Derbend.

The Second Arab Campaign

Under Caliph Osman the Azerbaijanis revolted and refused to pay annual tributes. A large army was immediately assembled and dispatched under the command of Velid ibn Ugbe. The Arabs successfully spread rumors and stories about the invincibility of their armies. This was one of the reasons that the rebels surrendered without much fight. Velid renewed the Arab control of Azerbaijan.

The Third Arab Campaign

As soon as the hostilities between the Arabs and the Byzantine ended Selman ibn Rebiyye was appointed the commander of an expeditionary force to be sent to Georgia. On his way to Georgia, he entered Azerbaijan and arrived in the city of Beylegan. The residents offered him valuable gifts suing for peace. They also pledged to pay annual tributes. The Arabs continued to Barda and concluded a peace treaty with that city as well. Selman collected a great deal of wealth here which was later distributed among his soldiers. The next stop of the Arab army was Behrvar[11].

The tribute was agreed on in this city too. Then Selman moved on to Shirvan. The khan of Shirvan sent many gifts and offered peace. Then Selman marched to Deylem and Teberistan. He returned to the Azerbaijani city of Shabran[12]. It was that time that the Khazar army set up a camp in Shabran. No sooner had they heard about the Arab advance than their army retreated to the North Caucasus. The Arabs put up the tents near Bilenjer[13].

The story goes that one day a Khazar wounded and killed an Arab who was swimming in the river. The "hunter" brought the head of the Arab to his Khagan (ruler) disproving the legends that Arabs were immortal and invincible. The Khazars immediately attacked the Arabs and despite the

---

[11] A city in Mughan, Azerbaijan

[12] A city to the west of Derbend and Shemakha, Azerbaijan

[13] A city near Derbend, in the south of modern Russian Federation

fierce resistance of Selman's small army annihilated the Arab forces. Nowadays the place where they were massacred is a cemetery known as "The Forty". Habib ibn Muslime was ordered to revenge the Khazars for the death of Selman.

The Khazar Raids

The Khazars had been raiding Azerbaijani cities for centuries. In year 626, the Khazars assisted Byzantium troops in their defeat of an Iranian army near Neyneva[14]. The Khazars captured the cross taken by the Iranians from Girs Khalil and gave it to Byzantium. Khazars plundered Tiflis, Mughan and Shirvan on their way back home. Arabs appointed a certain Abdulrahman to subdue the Khazars. Later another Arab commander Selman ibn Rebiyye fought Khazars as we described earlier. His army perished near Derbend. In 729, Jerah ibn Abdullah led a huge army against the Khazars in Derbend and routed them. However, the Khazars regrouped after this defeat and drafted new forces to fight the Arabs. They clashed with the Arab forces where Kura and Arax rivers meet and crushed the Arab forces killing Jerah ibn Abdullah. The following year another Arab army under Said ibn Omer Al Harashi launched a new offensive against the Khazars. His troops moved via Erzurum, Ehlat and Barda and seized most of the Azerbaijani fortresses releasing many people imprisoned by the Khazars. The Arab army managed to thwart a counteroffensive led by the Khazar Khagan's son Taryel. In 732, Muslume ibn Abdulmelik was in charge of a military campaign against the Khazars. In order to cut off the Khazars from the support among the locals, Muslume had forty thousand migrant Arabs settle around Derbend. The Khazars, meanwhile, took advantage of an uprising of the Shirvan population against the Arabs and occupied Azerbaijan taking prisoner almost one hundred thousand people. The Khazars also rose to help Babek's resistance movement, but their efforts were frustrated by Afshin and Bugha, the commanders invited from Turan[15] to subjugate Azerbaijan.

The Arab Viceroys in Azerbaijan

Azerbaijan was completely integrated into the vast Islamic empire in 643. The Arabs governed Azerbaijan through appointed viceroys. These

---

[14] Neyneva's ruins still remain on the left bank of the Tigris River to the west of Mosul, in present-day Iraq
[15] Turan is an ancient name for Turkestan or today's Central Asia (The publisher's note)

appointees were headquartered in Tabriz. Although Barda was much larger than Tabriz, the latter's geographic location was more favorable as a capital city.

The Arabs collected taxes in Azerbaijan on an annual basis. The exact amount is not known apart from the Shirvan province that was known to pay two hundred thousand dirhams a year.

Under the Umevids Azerbaijan and Kurdistan were united into one province called Jezire and were ruled by one viceroy. Mehi ibn Bermek was appointed a viceroy in 775.

In 808, the rebellion of the residents of Khurram[16] was crushed by Caliph Harun Ar Rashid. In 816, a warrior by the name of Babek began a large-scale rebellion against the Arab rule. This revolt continued until 835 as all the efforts of the Abbasid Dynasty to quell it failed. Only in 835 did Caliph Al Motesimbillah invite a Turk from Turan by the name of Afshin to defeat Babek. These campaigns led to significant casualties on both sides. (See the previous sections on Babek and Afshin).

Babek's Castle in East Azerbaijan, Iran

In 837, Manekjur, a relative of Afshin was sent to Azerbaijan as the sovereign. However, Manekjur's loyalty to the Arabs came under suspicion two years later, and he was arrested by special Arab troops sent to Azerbaijan.

In 839, Ibn Al Bais who fought in Babek's army escaped from an Arab prison and launched another rebellion in Azerbaijan. The Abbasid viceroys attempted to forge an army from the Turkestani Turks again, but they were defeated this time. At last, the famous Turkic general Bugha was invited by the Arabs. Bugha, a Turk himself, surrounded Ibn Al Bais in Merend and captured him. Ibn Al Bais died in prison.

---

[16] This city was near Tabriz; it was also called Khurremabad

In 850, Caliph Al Mutevekkil Eliyullah made his son Moghre the ruler of Azerbaijan.

In short, Azerbaijan was ruled in this manner by the Arab viceroys from 643 to 926. Between 926 and 1029, Azerbaijan was under the control of Deysem ibn Salar and other viceroys, but little data are available about this period of our history. From 1029 to 1048, the Turkic Oghuz tribes launched several invasions into Azerbaijan, but local Khan Vehsudan and others repulsed their attacks.

The Conditions of the Conquered Nations under the Arab Rule

The nations that had suffered immensely throughout their history accepted the Muslim Arabs and their government without much resistance. These peoples found refuge in the Arab benevolence from the threats and pressures of Byzantium and Iran. The Iranians were spreading Zoroastrianism forcefully wherever they went. The Arabs, on the contrary, did not impose their religion upon others. They were content with the tributes the conquered peoples were paying. According to some Georgian sources Christianity became more widespread in Georgia under the Arab control than before. The Arabs saved Georgia from the threat of Zoroastrianism only after they had occupied Iran: This event contributed to the expansion of Christianity in Georgia[17].

The Seljuk Kingdom, 1053-1145
The Seljuks

The Seljuk tribes originated from Turkestan. One of the chiefs of the nomadic Seljuk tribes was Dugag. This Turkic tribe worshipped celestial stars and fire. Seljuk bey was the name of Dugag's son. Because of continuous wars in Central Asia Dugag along with two thousand people migrated to Iran and accepted Islam in 1057. Seljuk bey who became the chief after his father's death was believed to live one hundred years and had three sons: Arslan, Mikayil and Musa[18]. Dugag's sons conquered and ruled Iran and Bukhara.

Despite great conquests by Dugag's sons, his grandson, Arslan's son Toghrul is considered the founder of the Seljuk kingdom. Toghrul seized Merv and Nishabur. In 1038, he ousted the Gaznevids from Nishabur and was crowned the king. During

---

[17] This was noted in the book by A. Tumanski in 1910.
[18] Other sources claim Dugag had four sons (The publisher's note)

his reign Toghrul conquered Khorasan, Iran and Iraq and threatened the throne of the Abbasids.

The Seljuks conquered Azerbaijan in 1033. In 1054, the Azerbaijan provinces of Irevan[19] and Shirvan came under his control as well. In 1063, the Seljuks captured Georgia and Abkhazia and went to war with the Khazars. The Seljuks also expanded their possessions in Byzantium, India, and China. Such great kings as Alp Arslan and Melik Shah descended from the Seljuk dynasty. They were great patrons of art and sciences. Under their rule, several new roads and buildings were constructed. This Turkic dynasty also promoted literature and philosophy. Regrettably, at later stages of their rule the internal power strife considerably weakened the state, and soon it disintegrated into smaller states called Atabegs and Khanates. These Seljuks were known in history as the Iranian Seljuks in order to distinguish them from the ones who remained in Central Asia. At the same time, the Seljuk Turks founded two other states in Byzantium and Kerman. Those groups came to be known as the Rum Seljuks and Kerman Seljuks, respectively. We are not going to dwell on the history of those tribes as they did not play a major role in the history of Azerbaijan.

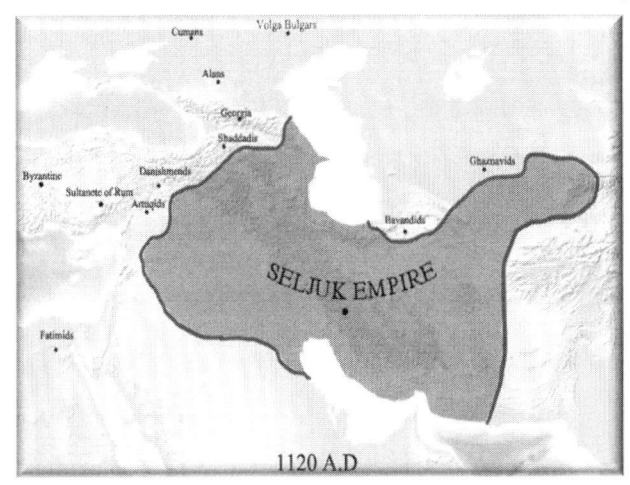

Map of the Seljuk Territories

The Sultans of the Iranian or Azerbaijani Seljuks

1. Toghrul bey ibn Arslan ibn Seljuk (1038)
2. Alp Arslan ibn Chagri bey ibn Mikayil (1063)
3. Melik Shah ibn Alp Arslan (1072)
4. Barkuyarig ibn Melik Shah (1082)
5. Mohammed ibn Melik Shah (1104)
6. Sanjar ibn Melik Shah (1117)

---

[19] Also known as Yerevan, currently in the Republic of Armenia (The publisher's note)

7. Mahmud ibn Mohammed (1117)
8. Toghrul II ibn Tapar (1131)
9. Mesud ibn Mohammed (1134)
10. Melik Shah II ibn Barkuyarig (1152)
11. Mohammed II ibn Mahmud II (1152)
12. Suleyman Shah ibn Mohammed I (1160)
13. Qizil Arslan ibn Toghrul II (1161)
14. Toghrul III ibn Arslan.(1175-1193)

The Seljuk Administration

By 1054 entire Azerbaijan was under the Seljuk rule. The Seljuks governed Azerbaijan via local khans. Starting from 1117 the Seljuks began appointing their own khans, governors, and thus, were running the country through a direct rule. In 1131, emir Chaveli bey was appointed a viceroy to the Aran province in Azerbaijan. In 1145, Chaveli bey seceded from the already weakened Seljuk empire and founded an independent Azerbaijani government. After his death, Shemseddin Eldeghiz took over and declared an independent Azerbaijani state with its capital in Ganja.

PART TWO

The Independent Atabeg State 1146-1409

The General Situation in Azerbaijan

In 1146, the Turks created an independent Azerbaijan State. The Ottoman government did not emerge yet. Asia Minor was controlled by the Rum Seljuks, Iran by the Iranian Seljuks. Turkestan was dominated by the Khorezmshahs. Russia consisted of only Moscow province, and Istanbul was still Byzantine. As far as Armenia is concerned as we stated earlier this country was not on the international political stage at all. The only reminder of Armenians was Nasireddin Sugrrian Sani who ran the affairs in Ehlat under the title of Armenshah. Georgia was a semi-independent state.

The new Turkic government in Azerbaijan was called the Atabeg State. Atabeg means "fatherly lord" in Azerbaijani. Atabeg was the title of the tutors and mentors of Seljuk princes. The first Azerbaijani ruler Shemseddin Eldegiz was called so because of his previous profession. After the establishment of the independent state, Eldegiz resolved not to borrow the Seljuk titles of Sultan or Khagan but keep the simple title of Atabeg. In the beginning, the capital of the newly founded Azerbaijani state was Ganja then it was moved to Shemakha. Finally, Tabriz was selected as the capital city. A Khutbah, a ceremonial prayer praising an important statesman or event, was recited in his name thus crowning him as the sovereign of Azerbaijan. He ordered the first coins of independent Azerbaijan to be minted that year.

The Atabeg State

Atabeg Eldegiz[20]

Shemseddin Eldegiz founded the Atabeg state in Azerbaijan and ruled it from 1146 to 1172. He earned the title Atabeg the Great. Eldegiz used to be a vizier of the Seljuk sultan Mahmud. He was also a mentor of an adopted son of Sultan Toghrul ibn Mahmud. Later Eldegiz was appointed the viceroy to the Aran province of Azerbaijan. Later on, he annexed other parts of Azerbaijan and established a unified Azerbaijan state. This state became very powerful within a short period of time. It was providing political, economic, and military assistance to the neighboring countries as well. For instance, in 1161, Eldegiz responded to the Hamadan ruler Suleyman's request for military assistance in a war with his neighbor Asian Shah by leading the Azerbaijani troops against Asian Shah and routing him. In 1171, Eldegiz captured the city of Rey and incorporated it into Azerbaijan. In his last years, he marched to the northwest of the Caucasus[21] and conquered Tiflis and Georgia. On his way home, he caught

---

[20] Eldegiz served at the court of Seljuk Sultan Mesud. The Sultan was extremely happy with his services and always benefited from Eldegiz's talent and intellect. Sultan Mesud arranged the marriage of his niece and Eldegiz. This woman gave birth to two sons Mohammed and Qizil Arslan. Eldegiz's contribution to his lord was immeasurable. Eldegiz led the Seljuk armies in the conquest of Baku, Ganja and Shirvan regions of Azerbaijan. Sultan Mesud died of the wound he suffered during a hunt. A palace power struggle ensued which led to a power vacuum in the Seljuk kingdom. Eldegiz acted fast to enthrone Mesud's son Toghrul from Revanduz. Toghrul was content with the title itself and did not interfere with state affairs at all entrusting Eldegiz to run the country. Eldegiz married Toghrul's mother and had full control of the nation. After Toghrul's mother deceased Eldegiz incarcerated Toghrul and brought another prince Arslan to power. Arslan's mother Tarikh Khatun also married Eldegiz. As in Toghrul's case Eldegiz was the true king of Azerbaijan. As a result of Eldegiz's wise and astute leadership, Azerbaijan secured the borders of the country and even expanded the territories controlled by Azerbaijan.

[21] The Caucasus (Gafgaz in Azerbaijani) means a horse in archaic Persian (asb or as). The tribes that bred horses were known as "a-as" or "a-asi", and those who lived in mountainous areas were called "ruh-as" or "kav-as". The words "Asia" and "Caucasus" originate from that root. In ancient times the mountains between India and China were named Caucasus. The warriors of Alexander the Great who marched to India mentioned those mountains as the Caucasus. The Roman historian Polibi called those mountains Caucasus 800 years before Mohammed's migration to Mecca. Even in the Middle Ages a Christian Missionary by the name of Dezideri called the Tibet mountains the Caucasus. The belief is that the peoples who migrated from Central Asia

typhus and died in the city of Nakhichevan in 1172. This great Azerbaijani leader was buried in a famous mosque in Hamadan which had been built by himself.

Atabeg Mohammed (Jahan Pehlevan)

Atabeg Mohammed was crowned in 1172. He became the greatest and most famous of the Atabegs commanding the respect of all the rulers of Iran and Turan. The Abbasid Dynasty in Baghdad recognized only two governments: the Syrian ruler Selaheddin Eyyubid and his highness Atabeg Mohammed in Azerbaijan. The Caliph demonstrated his respect and attention to Atabeg Mohammed more than to Selaheddin by ordering ceremonial prayers in Mohammed's name. The Caliph would send many gifts to Atabeg Mohammed and repeatedly bestowed noble titles upon him.

During Mohammed's first years Tabriz and Maragha were occupied by the Uzbeks from Central Asia. Atabeg defeated the invaders and liberated those Azerbaijani cities. Atabeg made every effort to secure stability and prosperity in the country as well as peace with foreign countries. He established good relations with the Caliph in Baghdad. His ties with Ehlat were dramatically improved after his daughter married the ruler of Ehlat. Mohammed also laid the foundation for friendly relations with Egypt. The historical documents claim that the Atabeg was a very capable, peace-loving, and influential ruler. In 1186 he was treacherously assassinated by a certain Abu Yehya. He left four sons Gutleg Inanj, Mir Miran, Abubekr and Ozbek. His brother Qizil Arslan *(Red or Golden Arslan, the publisher's note)* became the king after Mohammed's death.

---

to the west transferred that name to the mountains in the region between the Black and Caspian Seas because of its similarity to the terrain in that part of Central Asia. It is noteworthy that the local peoples of the Caucasus call the mountains by different names: some Azerbaijanis call it Fit Dagi (literally Whistle Mountain), Circassians - Gazi Bey (a male name), Ossetians - Gurju (literally Georgian), Nugays - Ulduz Dagi (literally Star Mountain). The Arabs used to call it Jebel ul Kit, Jebel ul Gayif. The Ottomans and others knew it as "Kuhi-gaf. Gaf or Gapf means Gehbe (means a whore in many languages). Historians suppose that these mountains bear the name "Gaf" because of the ancient and powerful amazon country that used to be on the Caucasian mountains. Amazon means "hemezen" that is a woman or female in Farsi.

Qizil Arslan (1186-1190)

The Sultans

The Abbasids who ruled in Baghdad despised the Seljuks in Iran who were already very docile. Caliph Al Nasredinullah used Qizil Arslan to defeat the last Seljuk emperor in Iran. The reign of Toghrul, the Seljuk sovereign in Iran, came to an end when Qizil Arslan had him killed. In return for this service, the Caliph honored Qizil Arslan with the title of Sultan. After this event, the Azerbaijani Atabegs began holding high ranking positions in the Caliph's palace and enjoy special privileges in the Islamic world. The Azerbaijanis were the only ones to have the right to bear the title Sultan after the Seljuks. Thus, the Atabegs began to be called Sultans after they had earned it with their blood.

Sultan Qizil Arslan

One of the great Turkic women who played an important role in our history was Atabeg Mohammed's wife Getibe Khatun. She was deeply involved in the state affairs of Azerbaijan. Thus, after Atabeg Mohammed's assassination, Getibe Khatun attempted to marry the Seljuk Prince Toghrul in order to bring Gutlug Inanj to power. However, Qizil Arslan immediately marched to Hamadan and married Getibe Khatun himself.

Toghrul was incited by his close advisor by the name of Zehr to revolt against Azerbaijan claiming that " ... you are the legitimate ruler of Iraq and only capable sultan among the Seljuks. Qizil Arslan annexed Iraq to Azerbaijan unjustly". Toghrul put together an army to fight Azerbaijan and after several battles in Mazandaran, Damghan and Hamadan he was defeated and thrown into a dungeon in Kehran castle.

The Caliph himself as we mentioned above assisted Qizil Arslan in this war. However, Qizil Arslan was later tragically assassinated. Although the murderer remained unknown, he was said to belong to the sect of the Batinids[22].

It is also suspected that the Iraqi emirs had a role in his assassination. The Iraqis fought alongside Qizil Arslan against their own ruler Toghrul. Naturally, they knew that Qizil Arslan would never trust the people who betrayed their own lord. That is why they may have helped kill Arslan.

---

[22] The Batinids - read about the Ismailids in the section about Hulagu Khan

Nevertheless, the Azerbaijanis had no difficulty in crushing all these revolts and incorporating Hamadan into Azerbaijan again.

Atabeg Abubekr (Nusretddin), 1191-1210

In 1191, Arslan's nephew Abubekr ascended to the throne. He usurped all the power by sending his brother Gutlug Inanj to Iraq as the viceroy. It was precisely this time when Toghrul escaped from the prison and began stirring trouble in Iraq. Gutlug requested military assistance from Atabeg Abubekr who denied it. Gutlug reentered Iraq with the help of the Khorezmshahs. Several skirmishes took place. In the end, Gutlug attempted to assassinate Toghrul by poisoning him. Gutlug involved his own mother Getibe Khatun in his effort. Getibe Khatun was supposed to serve a poisoned food to Toghrul. Toghrul, on the other hand, discovered the plot and forced Getibe Khatun to eat the deadly food herself. The lady died at once. Gutlug Inanj was thrown into a dungeon. Then Gutlug Inanj broke out of the prison and flee to Azerbaijan. But because of many differences between him and his brother Atabeg Abubekr they quarreled. Their growing differences led to four armed clashes between the brothers. Abubekr won all of them.

Abubekr was a terrible debaucher neglecting all the state affairs. He became a pathetic figure. As we stated above, he did not render any help to his brother in Iraq. During his rule, the mayors of Maragha and Ardabil revolted against him. The rebellion was suppressed with enormous difficulties. Then, the Georgians attacked Azerbaijan who were repulsed after some Azerbaijani nobles from the royal court married Georgian noble ladies. Abubekr died in 1210.

Atabeg Ozbek (Muzeffereddin) 1210-1225

Abubekr's brother Ozbek replaced him in 1210. But under his reign, even more aggressors targeted Azerbaijan for he was as feeble and drunk as his late brother. The discipline in the army and in the palace was at its lowest. Aydoghmush, the mayor of Hamadan, attacked Azerbaijan but was beaten back by Ozbek's commander Minkuli. Minkuli chased Aydoghmush all the way to Hamadan. Minkuli took over Hamadan. In the wars that ensued Minkuli finally killed Aydoghmush.

Caliph Al Nasireddin urged Atabeg Ozbek, the Batinid leader Jelaleddin and Erbil ruler Muzeffereddin Kovkubra to storm Minkuli jointly. Minkuli was defeated by this huge army, and Hamadan was divided between Azerbaijan and the Batinids. It is remarkable that in this operation the Caliph used the Batinids who were despised by the Caliph himself and the rest of the Islamic world.

Although Ozbek did expand the Azerbaijani possessions thanks to the help from the Caliph, he could not properly defend them because of his weaknesses that we have described above. Ozbek came under an attack of the Khorezmshahs in 1217 and the Mongols in 1220. In 1225 Jelaleddin Khorezmshah captured Tabriz effectively terminating Ozbek's rule.

Ozbek retreated to Ganja. Soon thereafter Jelaleddin occupied Ganja but allowed Ozbek to stay in Ganja. However, Ozbek's wife Mehri Jahan Khatun divorced Ozbek and married Jelaleddin. Right after this event, Ozbek died of grief in Ganja.

The Conquest by the Khorezms[23]
Jelaleddin Khorezmshah

Jelaleddin Khorezmshah annexed Iraq to Azerbaijan and ruled the latter from 1225 to 1230. Khoy, Selmas and Urmiyye were left under the jurisdiction of Meleke Khatun, the wife of Atabeg Ozbek. When Jelaleddin was on his Iraqi campaign, his vizier Sheref-ul-mulk tried to seize those cities from Meleke Khatun. Meleke's troops were surrounded in a place called Tela. But the prompt assistance of the Ehlat leader broke the siege, and Meleke Khatun was transported to Ehlat. Having abandoned this plan Sheref-ul-mulk attacked the city of Revanduz and demanded that the mayor of the city who was a woman[24] marry him. However, Jelaleddin

---

[23] The Khorezmshahs – the word derives from the name of Khorezm or Khive, a city in Central Asia. The Seljuk Sultan Melik Shah appointed a Turk by the name of Anush Tekin the viceroy to Khive. After Tekin's death, his son Mohammed assumed the post and took the title of Khorezmshah. A descendant from this dynasty by the name of Atsiz became obsessed with the idea of independence and subsequently was exiled from Khive. He returned to the city later and succeeded in carrying out his plans for independence. Atsiz's dynasty gave birth to such great kings as El Arlsan, Shah Mahmud, Tekish, Elaeddin, Jelaleddin all of whom carried the title of Khorezmshah. Under the last Khorezmshah Jelaleddin, Genghis Khan swept through Central Asia, and Jelaleddin had to flee to India. After two years of various adventures, Jelaleddin conquered Iran and Azerbaijan. He ruled those countries until the Tartar invasion in 1229.

[24] Our last Atabeg Ozbek had a son named Melik Khamush who later married Meleke Khatun, the mayor of Revanduz. Meleke Khatun gave Melik Khamush a very expensive and exquisite belt of the ancient Iranian Shah Keykavus. Melik presented this jewel-ornated belt to Jelaleddin who would wear it on special occasions. After Jelaleddin's defeat in 1229, the belt became a property of Genghis Khan's son. Melik Khamush fled to Alamut. The mayor of Revanduz was his wife, who later also married Jelaleddin.

traveled from Iraq to Revanduz and married this woman himself derailing Sheref's plans.

Sheref moved his troops to the wealthy Aran province of Azerbaijan. He imposed heavy taxes on the population. But soon he clashed with a maverick Syrian general who defeated Sheref. The Syrian general Ali Al Hajib chased Sheref to Merend. Sheref had to find refuge in Tabriz. Ali Al Hajib occupied Khoy, Nakhichevan and Merend and plundered those cities mercilessly.

Having spent the winter in Tabriz Sheref fought a battle with the Syrians at Nishabur. Sheref completely defeated the Syrian forces and rejected their peace offer. He threw the Syrians out of all the Azerbaijani cities and took over the cities of Khoy, Nakhichevan and Merend.

Meanwhile, Jelaleddin was engulfed by the domestic reforms after his Iraqi conquest. He moved his troops to Ehlat via Nakhichevan and besieged the city. After a long and brutal siege, Jelaleddin captured the city and destroyed the city leaving no stone upon another in 1228.

Jelaleddin began war preparations against the Seljuks from Konya and Syria known as the Rum Seljuks after the reports about their aggressive plans. He defeated the Seljuks in the city of Yasjimen[25], but later suffered defeats himself. Jelaleddin returned to Mughan in Central Azerbaijan. In his last years, he was repelling the onslaughts of the Tartars and even concluded a mutual assistance treaty with the Eyyubids to fend off the Tartars. In 1229 the Tartars *(The author refers to Mongol and Tartar armies, the publisher's note)* invaded Azerbaijan and routed Jelaleddin in Mughan. Jelaleddin was forced to retreat to Asia Minor for no ally came to help him. The Tartars ended the rule of the Atabegs and Khorezmshahs in Azerbaijan.

After his defeat in Mughan, Jelaleddin decided to migrate to Asia Minor. He was killed en route. It is suspected that he was assassinated by a Kurd whose brother had been hanged by Jelaleddin. The hero who was always victorious in his endless wars with India and Syria became a victim of a treacherous Kurdish guest of his.

---

[25] Yasjimen is believed to have been near the city of Kherpur.

Art and Education under the Atabegs

Art and education flourished under the Atabegs. Unfortunately, no monuments from that epoch remain today with the exception of Alinjig (Alinje) fortress to the west of Nakhichevan which was built by Qizil Arslan[26]. Regrettably, no archeological works have been conducted on this site either. The historians reckon that this fortress could hold jewelry and other precious metals since many Azerbaijani kings were hiding them in Alinje during foreign invasions. For instance, Melik Ashraf Jelairli, Sultan Ahmed and others are known to have stashed away their wealth in this fortress.

Momune Khatun Mausoleum, Nakhichevan, Azerbaijan Republic

In order to comprehend the historic importance of this fortress, it suffices to mention a twelve-year siege by Tamerlane the Lame who managed to seize the fortress only after the conflict among the defenders of the fortress had made a part of it vulnerable to Tamerlane's attack. The impregnability of this fortress is immortalized in Azerbaijani poetry too: "There was a huge fortress of Qizil Arslan the apex of which scraped the heaven".

It was under the independent Atabeg government that Azerbaijan gave rise to such world-renowned giants of literature as a great thinker and poet Sheikh Nizami Ganjavi, poets Abul Ula, Khagani, Feleki, Mujireddin Beylegani and others. These prominent masters of literature attest to the fact that strong and independent Azerbaijan also prided itself in highly-developed culture.

---

[26] Momine Khatun Mausoleum in Nakhchivan, Azerbaijani Republic, is believed to have been commissioned by Atabeg Jahan Pahlavan (The publisher's note)

PART THREE

The Mongols (Ilkhanids, Chobanids, Jelairids)

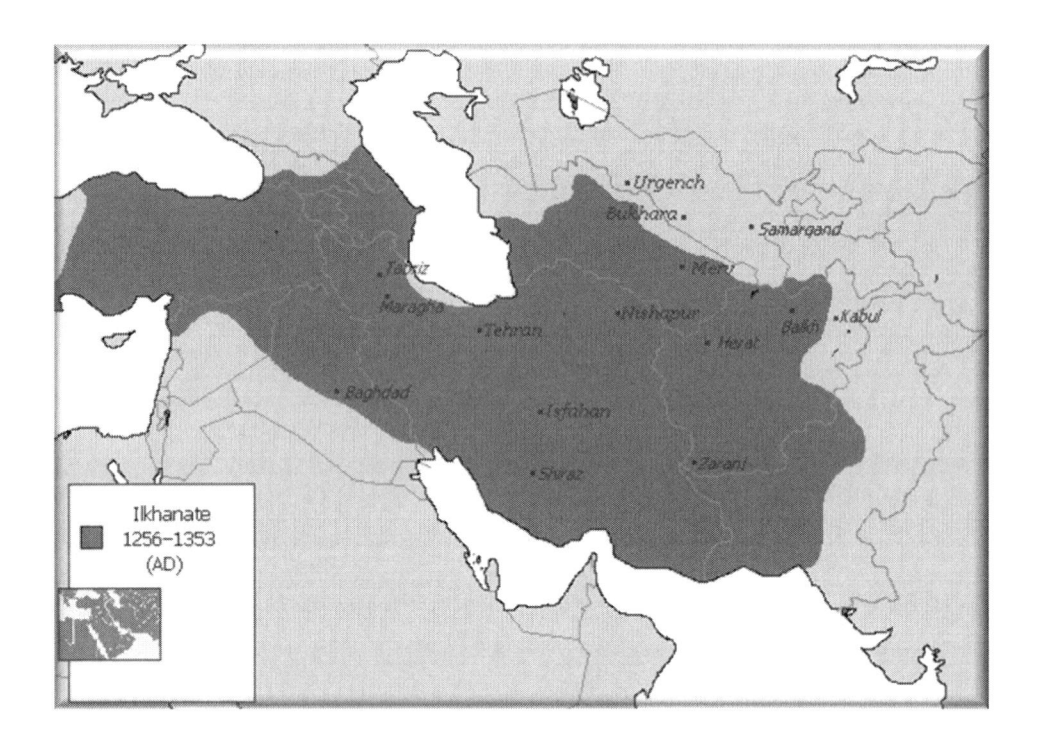

The First Mongol Invasion

The Mongols invaded Azerbaijan for the first time in 1214. During that campaign, the Mongols entered Azerbaijan through North Caucasus and occupied Azerbaijan up to the Georgian borders. The Georgian King Georgi the Fourth attempted to resist the Mongols but failed. The Mongols withdrew from the Caucasus for other reasons. Their withdrawal was accompanied by great losses inflicted upon the Mongols by the Azerbaijani Khan Behram khan. Soon the Mongols were back in Azerbaijan, but this time they concentrated around Ganja. The Mongols would invade and loot Azerbaijan regularly until Jelaleddin was defeated in Mughan. After that Mongol victory, they settled in Azerbaijan permanently.

The King of Iran and Turan

Timochin used to be a tribal chief in Mongolia and was a blacksmith by profession. In due course, he succeeded in separating a swath of land from China and Mongolia to create his own powerful state in Karakorum. Timochin took the title of Genghis which stood for a sea or ocean in Turkic and began an expansion in three directions: China, Russia, and Khorezm in Central Asia. However, after launching his massive campaigns he died in 1226. His generals followed his will and elected the most capable of them Ogtay Khan Khagan, their leader.

The Khagans

1. Genghis Khan (Timochin) (1164)
2. Ogtay Khagan ibn Genghis (1227)
3. Turakiya Khatun (his wife) (1231)
4. Kiyik Khan ibn Ogtay (1245)
5. Meiku Khan ibn Tuli ibn Genghis (1246)
6. Kublai Khagan ibn Tuli (1258)

Kublai Khan's reign can be considered the best era of the Mongols by far. Kublai Khan moved the capital from Karakorum to Beijing and appointed his brother Hulagu Khan the Ilkhan (ruler) in western Asia. Hulagu Khan in his turn occupied Iran and Azerbaijan and founded a strong Ilkhanate[27] with the capital in the Azerbaijani city of Maragha. Then he proceeded to conquer Iran, Iraq, Syria, Asia Minor, and the Caucasus that bordered Azerbaijan. After his death, the Ilkhanate remained under the control of his descendants. As time passed the Ilkhanate became an independent state. Genghis' offspring remained in and ruled Mongolia and China until 1333 and never had the honor of converting Islam. The Ilkhanids, however, converted to Islam and founded a vast Muslim state of Azerbaijan.

Ilkhanids - Hulaguids
Hulagu Khan 1255-1264

Hulagu Khan led his large army from Karakorum to Iran via Almalig, Samarkand crossing the Jeyhun river. He subdued all the principalities one by one and captured the fortress of Alamut liquidating the Ismaili tribe[28] (*also known as the Assassins*) in 1256. Hulagu Khan marched to Baghdad and rounded up the last Abbasid Caliph, Motesimbillah. Pars became independent. Hulagu had the Caliph and his entire family executed in Mongolia, then he returned to Azerbaijan. The new Ilkhanid government was established with the capital in Maragha. The Ilkhanids were to pay taxes to the Khaganate in Mongolia. But after several years Azerbaijan ended its relations with the Khaganate and stopped paying any tribute -becoming a completely independent country. Hulagu khan attacked Sham, Egypt, Mosul but went back to Maragha

---

[27] The Ilkhanids are known in history as the Iranian Mongols. This is a wrong definition since the only country critical to Mongols in their vast possessions from Khorasan to Asia Minor was Azerbaijan. The Ilkhanid capitals were also Azerbaijani cities of Maragha, Tabriz and Sultaniyye. Even the coins minted at that time said: "Minted in Azerbaijan". The book " Mirat ul buldani Nasiri" mentions the Ilkhanids as "the Azerbaijani government" with the center in Tabriz. That is why it will be more correct to call the Ilkhanids the Azerbaijani Mongols. Unfortunately, the Arab and other non-Azerbaijani historians constantly distort the facts to their own benefit. Besides, the Chobanids and Jelairids ruled only Azerbaijan with the exception of their occasional occupation of Iraq.

[28] The tribe of Ismailis, also known as the Batinids originated from the infamous sheykh Hasan Sabah. This tribe constructed nine fortresses with Alamut being one of them on the mountains of Qazvin. The Ismailis dispatched assassins all over the Islamic world to kill the prominent leaders and statesmen. Their endless bloodshed earned them the universal hatred of the Islamic world. The Seljuks sent several armies to eradicate this hated group of killers, but they failed to do so. Finally, the Mongols eliminated this threat to everybody thus doing a great service to humanity. The Batinids were originally supposed to be a group of Persians who fought against the Turks who ruled Iran. Later, however, they became a tool in the hands of any king who would pay them handsomely. This sect is a branch that broke away from Shiism, and one can encounter similar groups even today.

leaving his emir Kit Bugha in charge of those regions in 1259. Hulagu Khan was buried in Tabriz, Azerbaijan[29].

Abaga Khan 1264-1281

After Hulagu Khan's death, his son Abaga Khan ascended to power in 1264. A number of military conflicts took place during this khan's rule. Let us describe the main ones:

The Struggle with Bugay. Bugay, a descendant of Bati Khan invaded Azerbaijan from the north. The Ilkhan sent his brother Beshmut to counter this offensive. Beshmut forded the Kura River and defeated Bugay at the point called Jigha Muran. Bugay was killed, and the Kipchak plot to capture Shirvan and Derbend was derailed.

The Onslaught of Birke Khan. This Kipchak khan led his army into Azerbaijan to revenge his prior defeats. Abaga commanded the troops himself and fortified his position on the bank of the Kura River. The enemy stood on the other bank of the river for fourteen days and then attempted to ford the river near Tiflis (modern-day Tbilisi), but was repulsed. Birke Khan had to retreat. Abaga khan went back to Tabriz.

The war with Birag Khan. Birag Khan was a Turkestani khan who entered Khorasan via Samarkand and Merv. Abaga immediately marched to Khorasan and annihilated the invading force.

Abaga Khan was one of the greatest kings among the Ilkhanids. He was the first Azerbaijani emperor to establish diplomatic ties with some European countries. He married the daughter of the Byzantine emperor Pali Ulug, thus prompting the latter to send his ambassador to Tabriz. Other European countries followed the suit by sending their ambassadors to the Ilkhan's palace. Abaga Khan asked Kublai Khan to allow his daughter to marry Abaga's son Erghun. The Khagan agreed and sent his daughter to Tabriz. But Erghun had died before he arrived, and she married another son Gazan Khan. The convoy that accompanied Kublai Khan's daughter to Tabriz included Marco Polo, a famous European traveler. Abaga Khan died on his way to Sham after the news of his brother's defeat had reached him. It is suspected that he was poisoned (1281). Abaga Khan ruled the country for seventeen years.

---

[29] Hulagu Khan was buried on an island in Lake Urmiya, Azerbaijan (The publisher's note)

Tekudar Oghul (Ahmed Khan) 1282-1284

The congress convened after Abaga's death elected his brother Tekudar Oghul the emperor in 1282. Tekudar was secretly brought up and educated as a Christian. But he achieved nothing by this upbringing, and as soon as he became the king, he adopted Islam. Moreover, he took the name of Ahmed and began persecuting Christians which was not characteristic of our rulers. Ahmed Khan demolished many churches in Tabriz and hanged their priests.

Ahmed was never independent in his decisions. He was always under the influence of his emirs. Let me mention some of his most influential emirs:
- Supreme Chairman Khaje Sahib Divan
- His mother Kutun Khatun
- Sheikh Abdulrehman whom Ahmed called the father
- Sheikh Minkuli who called Ahmed his son.

Meanwhile, Tekudar's brother Erghun who was dreaming of the throne attempted a coup. He led a ragtag army called "Geravnas" from Khorasan but was defeated by Ahmed. Ahmed Khan also suppressed an uprising started by his other brother Gingurbay in the Mughan region of Azerbaijan.

Erghun did not abandon his plans to seize the crown of Azerbaijan. He enlisted an army in Khorasan and attacked the Ilkhan again. Tekudar sent his general Elyag to crush Erghun. However, a general by the name of Bugha betrayed Tekudar and switched sides during the battle. As a result, the commander was killed and Tekudar himself was captured. Erghun khan won that war and later at the demand of his brother Gingurbay's wife he had Ahmed Khan executed.

Erghun Khan

Abaga Khan's son Erghun was enthroned in 1284. Emir Bugha who was instrumental in bringing Erghun to power became the Grand Vizier. Bugha's influence became apparent even beyond the borders of Azerbaijan. He was honored with the title Chigh Sang by Kublai Khan. The title stood for a "grand chief" in Chinese. Erghun's orders would not take effect unless Bugha signed them. It was said that at some point Bugha even plotted to topple Erghun and install a person from the Hulagu dynasty.

However, Bugha's plans failed. Erghun khan had Bugha and his loyal troops liquidated in Mughan as soon as he was informed of the plot to overthrow him. Under Erghun khan, the Azerbaijani government protected the Christians. Dimitri, a Georgian prince, for example, was appointed a mayor of Ehlat. But Dmitri shared Bugha's fate since he was one of the plotters too. Bugha's death was followed by a dramatic reshuffle of the government that ended with the appointment of Sed ul Dovle as the Grand Vizier. Sed ul Dovle was Jewish and well known in Azerbaijan. The state coffer was put under his authority. It was not long, however, before this man was also hanged because of embezzlement and other corruption charges.

The Kipchak War. The Kipchak Tartars headed by Emir Burultay invaded Azerbaijan in 1289. The Ilkhan immediately ordered his commander Tighachari with his well-trained army to counter that aggression. Emir Choban was dispatched after Tighachari as a reinforcement. The Azerbaijani army destroyed the Kipchag forces in this war.

Tughanjig, a woman from Erghun's harem was suspected of black magic in order to become the Ilkhan's favorite wife. Erghun's reaction to this scheme was the execution of Tughanjig and all other women in the harem. Erghun died in 1289.

Keykhatu Khan 1290-1294

Erghun's death caused the nobles to split into two camps: one that backed the late khan's relative Baydu Khan from Baghdad, the other supported Erghun's brother Keykhatu khan. Keykhatu was savvier and quicker and took power in 1290.

The government was printing paper money at that time. This so-called silver paper money called "chav" was virtually worthless and was not popular in Azerbaijan where people were used to gold and silver coins. The lack of metal coins forced the government to print chavs. Keykhatu initiated this venture at the advice of a certain Al Umeyya. The chavs were used inside the country only, and travelers and businesspeople leaving the country were exchanging their chavs for gold and silver from the state treasury. The economic consequences of this monetary policy were ruinous. Commerce came to a standstill in Tabriz; shops shut down across the country and trade collapsed. Such poor economic conditions forced Keykhatu khan to abolish the chavs in Azerbaijan.

Internal Strife. The power struggle between Keykhatu's and Baydu's supporters got exacerbated as Baydu entered Azerbaijan with his

Baghdad emirs. Keykhatu ordered the arrest of his officers Khunjibala, Gushjisn and Aydajisn whom he suspected of having secret ties with Baydu. The two armies, meanwhile, clashed in Mughan. Keykhatu was defeated. He was later rounded up and beheaded together with his supporters. Baydu was immediately declared the Ilkhan in the city of Serab.

Baydu Khan 1294-1294

Baydu Khan's reign was short-lived. Keykhatu's nephew Gazan Khan was very angry at his uncle's death and determined to revenge. He revolted against Baydu leading "Garevnas" troops from Khorasan to Tabriz. Gazan Khan's troops included such brave and talented warriors as Gutlug shah and Novruz khan. During the war Baydu's close aide Toghachar went over to Gazan's camp. This betrayal led to a complete rout of Baydu's army. Baydu fled to Nakhichevan where his disloyal troops tied him up and handed him over to Gazan. Baydu's supporters Dogal, Eldar and others were picked up and liquidated one by one. Thus, Gazan became the new ruler of the country.

Gazan Mahmud Khan

When Erghun Khan's son Gazan became the king, he had not converted to Islam yet. Gazan khan appointed his general Gutlug shah who distinguished himself on the battlefield the commander in chief of the Azerbaijani army. Gazan Khan himself was married to an Armenian woman and always protected Christians. He swore to accept Islam on his victory over Baydu Khan. After his swift victory over Baydu Gazan khan converted to Islam with over one hundred thousand Tartars. He adopted the Muslim name of Mahmud. In order to commemorate his conversion to Islam Gazan Khan ordered his Vizier Khaje Alishah to construct a huge mosque in Tabriz in 1294. Only the ruins of this great Turkic monument known as "Ali shah's Mosque " remain in Tabriz today. Below are rebellions and wars that occurred during Gazan's reign.

Novruz Khan, one of Gazan's emirs began a mutiny in Khorasan that was ruthlessly suppressed by violent Gutlug Shah. Novruz Khan's entire family in Azerbaijan was annihilated.

Arslan Khan, a descendant of Genghis Khan, revolted against the Khan but was easily put down by Emir Choban.

Egyptian Campaigns. Gazan Khan undertook three military campaigns into Egypt in addition to putting down a number of revolts in

Asia Minor. During the first campaign, Gazan Khan led the troops himself and reached Damascus. The third campaign was commanded by Emir Choban. His forces clashed with Sultan Nasir's troops and were defeated. Choban had to retreat to Azerbaijan.

Gazan Khan was both a great warrior and statesman of his time. Gazan Khan refused to pay the already nominal tributes to the Khaganate and gradually became completely independent eliminating any foreign influence on Azerbaijan.

He was also an outstanding reformer. Under his rule, the justice department was established. Gazan also enacted special laws regulating taxation system, lands, and commerce. His abolishment of paper money and other popular actions that improved the population's well-being won him widespread support throughout the country. Gazan was a very wise and intelligent ruler who unfortunately did not live long. Alcoholism which was a big problem among Mongols in general took Gazan's life in 1303 too. He was buried in Tabriz's Shami Gazan mosque that had been built by himself. He made sure that the country was beautified during his rule. This Khan ordered the construction of the Tabriz Fortress Walls and such wonderful mosques as Shami Gazan and Rashidiyye.

Uljaytu Khan 1303-1316

Uljaytu ibn Erghun Khan was a Christian at the time of his crowning. After some time Uljaytu Khan became Muslim, took the name of Mohammed and the title of Khudabende. He eliminated any dissent and chaos, and restored stability and peace in the country. He became popular by being committed to the well-being of his subjects. This khan worked hard for the country founding the city of Sultaniyye in 1303. Uljaytu Khan ordered the transfer of the capital from Tabriz to Sultaniyye. He also initiated the construction of such cities as Sultanabad in Kurdistan and Uljaytuabad in the Mughan region of Azerbaijan. Below is the list of the wars that occurred during his rule:

The Gilan Campaign: He attacked the province of Gilan in his first military venture. Until that time the Turks had never entered Gilan. Gilan was marshland, and hence was never a priority for them. The Turks had their cattle graze in spring and spent the cold season in winter quarters. This was the primary reason that the Turks who dominated all parts of Iran had never cast their eyes on the marshlands of Gilan and Mazandaran. Georgia also did not become the subject of a Turkic invasion because of its terrain. Uljaytu imposed the tribute on conquered Gilan and returned to Azerbaijan. The famous general Gutlug Shah fell in this war.

The Sham Campaign: Uljaytu Khan moved against Sham in 1312 and captured the castle of Rehbe. He concluded a peace treaty with the Syrians and went back to Azerbaijan.

The Khorasan War: Chighatay khans Kebk and Yesutur seized and plundered Khorasan. Emir Ali Gushchu was sent to put an end to this aggression. Ali Gushchu routed the Chighatays and pursued them to the Azerbaijani borders. Yesutur had major disagreements with Kebk and found refuge in Azerbaijan. Kebk in his turn invaded Azerbaijan again. His aggression was repulsed this time too. Uljaytu Khan chose the Shiite branch of Islam when he converted. He ordered the names of Imams to be minted on the coins. This act won him broad support of Iranians most of whom were Shiites. Uljaytu Khan passed away in 1316 and was buried in "Kunbedi Sultaniyye" mosque (in Sultaniyye) built by himself.

Abu Said Bahadir Khan 1316-1335

A twelve-year-old Abu Said became the king after his father Uljaytu's death in 1316. Emir Choban, formerly a ruler of Khorasan, was the factual leader of the country. He moved his army to the north of Azerbaijan in a preemptive action against the Kipchaks. The Kipchaks gave up the idea to ford the Kura. At this time, a disagreement between Emir Choban on one side and Emir Gurmush and Emir Elyag on the other escalated into a full confrontation. The two armies clashed near Goyche Lake (also known as Sevan Lake). Emir Choban fled the battlefield, and the leaderless army returned to Tabriz. The army of two emirs entered and looted Nakhichevan. To counter this lawlessness the young Abu Said regrouped his troops and strengthened the discipline in his army. Abu Said's revamped troops attacked the enemy and wiped them out from Azerbaijan. This smashing military success at this young age earned Abu Said the nickname of Bahadir (a hero). Right after the war, Abu Said ordered the execution of Choban and his son. However, Choban's daughter Baghdad Khatun was married to Abu Said, and she revenged the death of her father by poisoning Abu Said. Thus, Abu Said died and was buried next to his father in Sultaniyye in 1335.

Horrible anarchy ensued after Abu Said's death and lasted until 1343. During those eight years, the Azerbaijani people saw eight sovereigns: Arpa, Musa, Mohammed, Togha Teymur, Jahan Teymur, Sati Beyim, Suleyman and Nushirevan. The chaotic situation continued under those kings, and none of them could stabilize the country. Those were the last of the Hulagu dynasty in Azerbaijan. After 1343 the country was run by the Chobanids, Jelairids, Muzefferids, Serbedars and other tribes.

The Chobanids (Sulduzi)

After several wars that occurred following the end of the Hulgu dynasty, Iraq including Baghdad came under the control of Sheikh Hasan Bozorg while Azerbaijan remained the kingdom of Sheikh Hasan Kichik[30]. Hasan Bozorg founded the Jelairid dynasty, and Hasan Kichik became the first ruler of the Chobanid dynasty. There was always a substantial gulf between those two governments. Hasan Bozorg was regularly invading Azerbaijan and was every time defeated by Hasan Kichik. But Hasan Kichik was soon murdered by his own wife Izzet Khatun[31]. His brother Melik Ashraf[32] came from Asia Minor to take the reins of power in Azerbaijan. But his cruel oppression of the people prompted locals to invite the Kipchag Tartars from Ezhderhan (today's Astrakhan in Russia). In 1355 the Kipchak chief Jani bey entered Tabriz without any resistance and hanged Melik Ashraf.

Azerbaijan came under the control of the Kipchak Turks, and the Chobanid rule in Azerbaijan came to an end. Sheikh Hasan Kichik and Melik Ashraf were buried in a mosque called "Master and Apprentice" in Tabriz.

---

[30] Sheikh Hasan Kichik ibn Teymurtash ibn Emir Choban descended from famous Emir Choban. The name of the dynasty derived from the name of the Emir. They were also called Sulduzi.

[31] Hasan Kichik's wife Izzet Khatun was rumored to have an affair with one of his emirs Yagub shah. After an unsuccessful war effort in Asia Minor Hasan Kichik repressed many of his emirs including Emir Yagub shah. Izzet Khatun was extremely worried and scared that the King could have found out about their secret love affair. That's why she colluded with one of the other women in the harem to murder Hasan Kichik. She supposedly squeezed the testicles of the King so strongly that he died on the spot

[32] As a result of Melik Ashraf's unjust and oppressive policies the common people were forced to leave Azerbaijan seeking the better life. Thus, the mayor of Barda famous Gazi Mehyeddin traveled to Ezhderhan (today's Astrakhan in Russia) to recount the horrors of everyday life in Azerbaijan to Jani bey. Jani bey swore to Gazi that he would rescue the people from that despot. Jani bey kept his promise and marched into Azerbaijan through Derbend. Ashraf immediately secured his treasury in the Alinjig Fortress and attempted to fight Jani bey. Nonetheless, his army fell apart even before he reached the frontline. Ashraf tried to escape with two men to Khoy where he finally surrendered to Jani bey. Ashraf was executed with great disgrace. Ashraf is said to have possessed enormous wealth. He adored precious metals especially gold. His love for gold has left its mark on our present lives too. A famous small gold coin still used (in 1923, The publisher's note) in Azerbaijan is called ashrafi in his honor.

The Jelairids (Ilkhanids) 1339-1409

The Jelairids were Tartars who originally settled in the Astarabad area when they reached Azerbaijan in the army of Genghis khan. Ilkhan was the name of one of Juji Tirmele's (their chieftain) generals. Ilkhan had nine sons. His son Agh Bugha's officer Hussein Gurkan was the father of Sheikh Hasan Bozorg.

Hasan Bozorg earned his fame during the rule of Uljaytu Khan. Hasan was honored with such high titles as Nuyan bey and Ulus bey usually given to prominent warriors. Under Abu Said Hasan married a daughter of Emir Choban thus gaining more political clout. Since then the power struggle was primarily between Hasan Bozorg and Hasan Kichik. Hasan Kichik arranged marriage of one of his commanders Suleyman with Sati beyim, a descendant from the Hulagu dynasty. Hasan's next step was to declare Suleyman the Khan. Hasan Bozorg immediately moved against him but was defeated at the battle of Maragha in 1339.

Sheikh Hasan Bozorg 1339-1355

Hasan Bozorg was governing Iraq including its capital Baghdad when Hasan Kichik attacked him. However, his offensive came to a halt to the west of Baghdad, and Hasan Kichik had to retreat to Azerbaijan. Only after the death of Hasan Kichik did Hasan Bozorg enter Tabriz but had to get out of the city on the news of Melik Ashraf's advance. In 1347 Melik Ashraf in his turn attempted to capture Baghdad by laying siege to it. His efforts failed. Hasan Bozorg died of natural causes in Iraq in 1355.

Sultan Hussein 1355-1357

Hussein, one of the five sons of Hasan Bozorg, became the sovereign of Iraq after Hasan's death. His other son Uveys fought the Kipchaks in Azerbaijan and in 1357 forced them to flee from Azerbaijan via Nakhichevan. Akhi Chugh, the Kipchak leader, invaded Azerbaijan again seizing the moment when the Jelairid Emirs were disobedient to the Khan. Uveys had to retreat to Baghdad. On the other hand, the Muzaffarids defeated Akhi Chugh and took over Tabriz. The Muzaffarid chief Mohammed left Tabriz as a huge army of Uveys approached the city. Uveys meanwhile charged into Akhi Chugh's forces routing them and killing Akhi Chugh. Consequently, Tabriz and the rest of Azerbaijan came under the Jelairid control.

Sheikh Uveys 1357-1372

Sheikh Uveys sat on the Azerbaijani throne and annexed Iraq after his brother Hussein died in Baghdad. He became known for his courage and fairness. The following events were the most important ones under his reign.

The Baghdad Uprising. In 1365 Khaje Merjan colluded with the Egyptian king and revolted against Azerbaijan by reading ceremonial prayers in the name of the Egyptian king. Uveys warned the Egyptian government not to give refuge to Merjan in case of his escape, then marched to Baghdad. Merjan was left without any assistance from Egypt and had to face the threat of the Azerbaijani troops by himself. He ordered to dig ditches around the city and fill them with water. Uveys was to stop at nothing and ordered his troops to ford the moat on boats. The city was easily put under the Azerbaijani control. Merjan was arrested, and his eyes were gouged.

The Campaign of Mosul. Uveys besieged Mosul in 1364. The mayor of Mosul Bayram Khoja of the Qaraqoyunlu dynasty was forced to flee. His attempt to retake the city with the support of Turkmen tribes was unsuccessful. Thus, Mosul was incorporated into Azerbaijan followed by the city of Mardin.

The Shirvan Operation. Sheikh Uveys instructed his General Behram bey to punish the Shirvan Khan Kavus ibn Keygubad who was regularly pillaging Karabakh and killing civilians there. In 1366 Behram bey besieged the Shemakha Fortress. A three-month-long siege flushed Kavus out. He was captured and sent to Baghdad under a military convoy. Later he was pardoned and allowed to return to his native Shirvan.

The war of Rey. In 1370 Emir Veli, one of Tugha Timur's emirs attacked the city of Rey which was under the Azerbaijani control. Sheikh Uveys rapidly responded to this aggression by defeating him at Rey. Uveys chased Veli to Simnan. The following year Uveys attacked Veli again, but this time he returned to Tabriz after a tragic accident that had taken his brother Sheikh Zahid's life in Ujan. Emir Veli took the advantage of the situation and looted the city of Save. The Muzaffarids aided Veli in his conflict with Uveys because their marriage proposal to Uveys' daughter had been previously rejected.

Sheikh Uveys enthroned his son Hussein when he was still well and healthy, and immersed himself in spiritual activities. Sheikh Uveys was buried in the Rashidiyye mosque in Tabriz.

Sultan Hussein Jelaleddin 1372-1382

Sheikh Uveys left five sons and one daughter. His son Hussein ruled both Azerbaijan and Iraq.

In 1375 Shah Shuja of the Muzaffarids attacked Tabriz to revenge for his past defeats at the hands of the Azerbaijanis. Sultan retreated to Baghdad which was ruled by his brother Ali. Reinforced by Ali's forces Hussein recaptured Tabriz and forced Shah Shuja to flee. Shah Shuja, however, seized Sultaniyye and ousted its mayor Sari Adil.

In 1377 the deteriorating relations between Hussein and his brother Ali resulted in Ali's separating Iraq from Azerbaijan. In 1382 the popular discontent with Hussein's rule culminated in the revolt by his other brother Ahmed from Basra. Ahmed occupied Tabriz and had Hussein executed. Ahmed was declared the king.

Sultan Ahmed 1382-1409

Sultan Ahmed entered Tabriz as his other brother Bayazid fled to Sultaniyye for the fear of being executed. Here Bayazid was declared the Shah of Azerbaijan by Sari (Yellow) Adil and was encouraged to move against Tabriz. Sultan Ahmed retreated to Baghdad facing the forces of Sari Adil. However, the dissent and chaos in Sari's army resulted in Sultan Ahmed's return to Tabriz. Bayazid and Sari Adil escaped from Tabriz.

The reign of Sultan Ahmed was very oppressive. The ·people were subjected to terrible tortures and taxes. The population had to appeal to his other brother, Shah Ali, to restore stability and normal life in Azerbaijan. Shah Ali wasted no time and led his troops to Tabriz. Sultan Ahmed's army clashed with Ali's forces at Heftrud. But Omer, one of Ahmed's commanders betrayed him. In the subsequent events, Sultan Ahmed was forced to find refuge in Nakhichevan.

Shortly afterward, Sultan Ahmed backed by the Qaraqoyunlu tribes fought Shah Ali at Ardebil. Although the Qaraqoyunlus withdrew their army from the battle, Sultan Ahmed defeated Ali's army and killed Shah Ali as well. He reinstalled himself as the ruler in Tabriz having eliminated all his opponents. Only Bayazid in Sultaniyye did continue to oppose him.

Sultan Ahmed resolved this problem killing two birds with one stone: pleasing the Muzzafarids, who resided in Sultaniyye and getting rid of Bayazid. Bayazid was appointed the viceroy in Sultaniyye by Shah Shuja. His rule was harsh, and the people happily surrendered the city to Sultan Ahmed. Bayazid was captured, and his eyes were burned out.

Meanwhile, Sari Adil was running the show in Fars. He took advantage of Sultan Ahmed's return to Tabriz and attacked Sultaniyye. He also sent his envoy by the name of Berseg to Baghdad. Berseg conspired with the mayor of Baghdad, Abdulmelik, and murdered blind Bayazid. The city was looted. They wrought a terrible havoc upon Baghdad. Finally, Sultan Ahmed launched an offensive and seized Baghdad executing Berseg. Later that year he had Sari Adil assassinated in Fars. He completely cleared his way to absolute power in Azerbaijan. It was that time Tamerlane the Lame appeared on the geopolitical stage.

There are many books written on wars Sultan Ahmed waged against Tamerlane and the Qaraqoyunlus. After his death, his nephew Shah Mahmud stood at the helm of power in Baghdad. However, the Qaraqoyunlus occupied the city in 1411 ending his rule. But his wife Tendu Sultan ruled the rest of the country from Khuzistan till 1415. After her death, different people from the Jelairids ran the government until 1427. That year the Qaraqoyunlus took the city and put an end to the Jelairid dynasty after killing Sultan Uveys. Sultan Uveys and Sultan Hussein were buried in the mosque of Rashidiyye in Tabriz.

The Azerbaijani coins minted under the Jelairids

The largest collection of the Jelairid coins in the world is housed in the Russian Hermitage Museum in St. Petersburg. The museum boasts 224 coins of the Jelairid period. Seven of them are gold, two are bronze, and the rest are made of silver. This Russian museum has considerably enriched its collection at the expense of Azerbaijan. For instance, in 1858 during the archeological excavations in the Azerbaijani city of Ordubad, the expedition unearthed 454 Jelairid coins among other valuable finds. The Russian viceroy to the Caucasus at the time initiated the creation of this collection by sending it to the Hermitage.

Here are the most important coins:

The name and title of the king (Place and date of mint)
As-Sultan ul-Adil Khallede Mulkehu, Shirvan (1349)
As-Sultan ul-Adil Khalledullah Mulkehu, Shirvan (1354)
As-Sultan Sheikh Uveys, Shabran (1360)
As-Sultan Sheikh Uveys Bahadir Khan Balcu, Tabriz (1360)
As-Sultan ul-Azim Sheikh Uveys Bahadir Khan, Tabriz (1362), Nakhichevan (1362)

Other coins were minted in the following cities: Ardebil, Baku, Barda, Alinjig, Khoy, Nakhichevan, Shemakha, Tabriz, Urmiyye and etc. These coins had the names of the Azerbaijani rulers, the place and the date of the mint on one side, the "La Ilahe Illelah, Mehemmedun Rasulillah" ("There is no God, but Allah, Mohammed is His Prophet") and the names of Abu Bekr, Omer, Osman and Ali on the other.

Architecture in Azerbaijan under the Mongol and Tartar rulers

The architecture in Azerbaijan flourished under the Ilkhanids. Hulagu Khan founded the city of Maragha and turned it into his political and cultural center. His efforts to contribute to the city's growth and prosperity were exceptional. Hulagu Khan was buried in this city.

The city of Tabriz also enjoyed the attention of its ruler Gazan Khan. In 1302 Gazan Khan had two magnificent fortresses "Shami-Gazan" and "Rashidiyye" erected that encircled Tabriz.

"Shami-Gazan". Gazan Khan had a famous fortress "Shami-Gazan" constructed in Tabriz in order to perpetuate his name in history. The place where the fortress used to be is still known in Tabriz as Shami-Gazan Mehelle (neighborhood). Gazan Khan ordered the construction of a palace, a mosque and many tall buildings that according to many historians no other architecture in the East could rival. Unfortunately, we can see only the ruins of those marvelous buildings today. People stole porcelain items that were used to decorate these buildings. The green domes of Gazagkhana and the German factory in Tabriz are made of the porcelain extracted from "Shami Gazan". The mosques that are located between the "Shami-Gazan" mehelle and the Devechi neighborhood of Tabriz are decorated with china taken from that fortress. Gazan Khan was buried in a mosque in Tabriz.

"Rashidiyye". Gazan Khan ordered the construction of this castle within the defense walls of Tabriz. It was named after his Grand Vizier Khaje Reshiddin as he supervised the construction of this complex. Only the ruins are seen where splendid buildings once used to tower over the city.

The Mosque of Ali Shah. This mosque was built by Gazan Khan in celebration of his conversion to Islam (Tabriz, 1294). His second Vizier Tajeddin Ali shah was in charge of the construction, hence the name of the mosque. Its minarets and domes are said to have been extremely tall. Although the Russians claim to have seen the tall domes of this mosque when they occupied Tabriz in 1826 today only the ruins are remaining.

The Mosque of Ali Shah in Tabriz, by Pascal Coste, the 19th century

Suleymaniyye Mosque is called the "Master and Apprentice" mosque in Tabriz. Its construction was ordered by Suleyman Khan from the Hulagu dynasty in 1339. Its original building fell into disrepair. But recently one of the Tabriz merchants repaired the mosque. The huge dome that remains from its original version still captures the admiration with its marvelous design. Suleyman Khan, Sheikh Hasan the Little and Melik Ashraf from the Chobanids were buried here.

The city of Sultaniyye. Uljaytu Khan founded this city and moved the capital from Tabriz to here in 1304. Sultaniyye made tremendous progress in architectural designs. The famous three big doors and a window pattern of the city's mosque amazed even the European travelers, among them the Frenchman Monsieur Ulyarus who claimed that there was no other design like this in the Orient.

Qiz Qalasi (The Maiden Tower). The famous building that is still intact in Baku was also built by Uljaytu Khan in 1314- 1316. It is believed to have been used for an early warning of an attack.

PART FOUR

The Independent Qaraqoyunlu and Aghqoyunlu States (1410-1501)

The Qaraqoyunlu Dynasty

The Turkmens[33]

Turkmen tribes settled in Asia Minor and to the north of the Tigris and Euphrates from ancient times. The states in Asia Minor were run by such Turkmen tribes as Zulgedriyye and Bani Ramazan. Finally, under Ilkhan Erghun two large Turkmen tribes settled to the north of the Tigris for good. The flag of one tribe had a black sheep on it while the other's flag carried a picture of a white sheep. The names of these tribes were derived from these insignia. The Qaraqoyunlu (*qara means black, qoyun means sheep in Turkic languages, the publisher's note*) tribe settled around Erzinjan-Sivas, while the Aghqoyunlus (*agh is white in Turkic, the publisher's note*) chose Mosul-Amed (the former name of Diyarbekir).

When the Turkmens arrived in the region there were small states here. However, the strong and warlike Turkmens wiped them out and soon became a strong entity. The Qaraqoyunlus occupied Azerbaijan in 1410 and made Tabriz their center. The Aghqoyunlus in their turn took over Iraq and declared Baghdad their eternal possession.

The Differences between the Tribes

Although both of these tribes were of Turkmen descent there were some differences between them. Their rulers took advantage of these differences in an attempt to subdue each other. Thus, during Tamerlane the Lame's aggression the Qaraqoyunlus fought against him, and their chief Qara Yusif had to retreat with his army to Anatolia that was under Sultan Bayazid. The Aghqoyunlus on the other hand supported Tamerlane. In return Qara Osman, the Aghqoyunlu leader, was left in power and enjoyed even larger privileges under Tamerlane.

Only after the Tartars had left did Qara Yusif return to Tabriz and fight Qara Osman at Galeyi er Rum. He pursued Osman all the way to Baghdad which was also captured and annexed to Azerbaijan.

---

[33] The Turks who live between the Caspian and the Amu Darya are called Turkmens. Since they were the first Turks to accept Islam they are also known as Turk-Iman, that is the Turk who is faithful

The Qaraqoyunlu Dynasty

After the death of Qaraqoyunlu King Qara Mohammed in Erzinjan in 1387, Qara Yusif took over. Since he became the ruler he came under constant attacks by Tamerlane. Qara Yusif ran the state till 1419. Here are some of the kings who belonged to this dynasty

Qara Mohammed ibn Bayram Khoja (1380)
Qara Yusif ibn Qara Mohammed (1389)
Iskender ibn Qara Yusif (1419)
Jahanshah ibn Qara Yusif (1437)
HasanAli ibn Jahanshah (1467)

The Military Campaigns of Tamerlane The Lame
The First Campaign 1355

Tamerlane emerged as a vicious warrior in Turkestan and soon conquered all of Turan and Iran. After occupying the Azerbaijani city of Sultaniyye he returned to his homeland.

The Second Invasion 1385

Tokhtamish who was appointed the viceroy of the Kipchak territories by Tamerlane occupied most of Russia and destroyed their capital Moscow. After this enormous success on the battlefield, he began considering the independence of his kingdom. Tokhtamish sent his envoys to Azerbaijan to meet with Ahmed Khan of the Jelairids in Tabriz. The purpose of this mission was to conclude a pact against Tamerlane. However, Ahmed Khan rejected the offer and hanged the envoys. Tokhtamish attacked Azerbaijan in 1384 and looted Tabriz in a punitive campaign. Tamerlane was extremely upset by these events. He entered Tabriz the following year without any resistance.

The Third Campaign 1392

Tamerlane attacked Iraq after his successful completion of a Shiraz campaign. He forced Ahmed Khan of the Jelairids, who was also the ruler in Baghdad to flee to Egypt. Tamerlane occupied Iraq and launched offensives into Kurdistan and Georgia. At the same time, he moved his army to counter Tokhtamish's troops after having been informed of the latter's intentions to seize Azerbaijan. Tamerlane routed Tokhtamish at the Terek river in 1394.

This was the second defeat of Tokhtamish at Tamerlane's hands. Tokhtamish escaped and found refuge at the palace of the Lithuanian king. Seven years later he was assassinated by an unknown person. Tamerlane appointed another person the ruler of the Kipchak lands. He subdued Georgia and after arranging a raid along the Itil river (*today's Volga river in Russia, the publisher's note*) returned to Samarkand. His son Miran Shah was left in Azerbaijan and Iran as the sovereign. Tamerlane's return home resulted in the comeback of many previous chieftains. Thus, Qara Yusif returned to Tabriz, Ahmed Khan was back in Baghdad and others followed the suit.

The Fourth Campaign 1399

Tamerlane undertook a successful campaign to India. Then he entered Azerbaijan again. Qara Yusif had to withdraw his forces to Anatolia which was under Ottoman Sultan Bayazid. As Tamerlane advanced the small principalities who were subdued by the Ottomans joined Tamerlane's army. The relations between Bayazid and Tamerlane quickly worsened. Bayazid's seizure of Sivas angered Tamerlane even further. Meanwhile, Tamerlane launched another raid, this time into Syria through Georgia. He signed a peace accord with the Egyptians and went back to Baghdad. Here Faraj, the sovereign appointed by the Jelairids could not resist Tamerlane who himself organized and led the army. Tamerlane took the city and settled in Karabakh for the winter.

It was then that Bayazid captured Erzinjan. At the same time, Qara Yusif took over Tabriz again while Ahmed Khan became the ruler of Baghdad. After the long correspondence between Tamerlane and Bayazid, they took up arms. The war at Ankara in 1401 ended with a defeat of Bayazid. Meanwhile, Qara Yusif moved from Tabriz to Baghdad and took the power from Ahmed Khan who fled the city. Tamerlane had only one enemy left in the whole region, the Azerbaijani King Qara Yusif. Their forces clashed in 1403. Qara Yusif was defeated and forced to retreat to Syria. Ahmed Khan was also in Syria at that time. Both of these Azerbaijani kings were jailed.

Tamerlane went back to his native Samarkand to prepare for a massive campaign into China. However, Tamerlane died on his way to China. Right after his death Qara Yusif immediately returned to

Azerbaijan and claimed the throne. Most Turkmen Emirs pledged their allegiance to him.

Tamerlane's Descendants

Tamerlane the Lame (1369)
Khalil ibn Miran Shah ibn Tamerlane (1404)
Shahrukh ibn Tamerlane (1408)
Ulugh bey ibn Shahrukh (1445)
Abdullatif ibn Ibrahim ibn Shahrukh (1449)
Abu Said ibn Mohammed ibn Miran shah (1450)
Mirze Yadigar ibn Mohammed ibn Baysungar ibn Shahrukh (1468)
Hussein BayQara ibn Mensur ibn BayQara ibn Sheikh Omer (1470)
Badi-uz-zeman and Mirze Muzzeffer (1505-1507)

Tamerlane's vast empire was doomed after his death. The local chieftains who had fled in the face of Tamerlane's advance returned to their homelands and claimed the power. Only Iran did stay under the control of Tamerlane's descendants until the emergence of Shah Ismail the First of the Safavids. Khorezm was another country that was controlled by the Tamerlaneids. Later Babur Khan, one of the Khorezm khans marched to India and created a famous Turkic state known as "The Great Mogul State". The Turks were the rulers of India until the English came to dominate India.

Yusif Shah (Qara Yusif) 1406-1419

After Tamerlane's death, Miran shah who was appointed the sovereign of Iran had to defend his title from local warlords. Under such circumstances Qara Yusif took Diyarbekir, and the Jelairids seized Baghdad. In 1405 Miran shah's son Abubekr Mirze led quite a large army against Ahmed Khan who controlled Baghdad. On the other hand, Qara Yusif attacked Miran shah and fought his army at the banks of the Arax river. Qara Yusif defeated Miran shah's army and killed Miran shah himself. Encouraged by this military success Qara Yusif decided to destroy Abubekr Mirze too. He caught up with Abubekr's troops in Nakhichevan and completely vanquished them.

After this battle, Qara Yusif put all of Azerbaijan under his control. In 1409 Qara Yusif attacked and defeated the Aghqoyunlus. Meanwhile seizing the opportunity Ahmed Khan launched an offensive against Tabriz.

It is noteworthy that after the defeat of the Western Turks at the hands of Tamerlane at Ankara both Qara Yusif and Ahmed Khan escaped to Egypt. There they were arrested and thrown in jail by the Egyptian king. Both of these Azerbaijani rulers swore not to fight each other when they returned to the motherland. Now it was Ahmed Khan who broke the promise and tried to capture Tabriz. Qara Yusif fought a bloody battle with Ahmed Khan and won. Ahmed Khan was killed when he tried to flee the battlefield. In 1410 Qara Yusif annexed Baghdad to Azerbaijan again. His son Shah Mohammed became the viceroy of Baghdad. Qara Yusif himself undertook another campaign against the Aghqoyunlus. This time he did not succeed. After a long siege of the Arghani Fortress, he gave up and returned to Azerbaijan.

The Shirvan Campaign 1412

During the conflict between Tamerlane and the Qaraqoyunlus, the Khan of Shirvan Sheikh Ibrahim Khan supported Tamerlane and sent his troops towards Tabriz. They set up a camp near the city. However, the Qaraqoyunlus attacked the camp unexpectedly and captured Ibrahim's son Keyumers who commanded the expedition. No sooner had this adventure failed than Ibrahim Khan immediately sent a special envoy with precious gifts to Tabriz asking to spare his beloved son's life. Qara Yusif released his son only after having obtained assurances from Ibrahim that he would never act against Qara Yusif again. But it was not long before Ibrahim allied himself with Georgian king Constantin against Qara Yusif. Ibrahim had his son Keyumers murdered since Keyumers had refused to fight the Qaraqoyunlus. Ibrahim and Constantin's troops made their way towards Tabriz. Qara Yusif dispatched his commander Baba Haji with elite forces to counter the advancing Shirvan-Georgian forces. Qara himself marched to Karabakh. En route to Karabakh, the Mughan, Nakhichevan and other Turkic tribes joined Qara's troops. The Qaraqoyunlus and their allies forded the Kura river and rammed into the Shirvan army. The Shirvanis were utterly defeated. To Qara Yusif's surprise, the Georgians attempted to put up a fight. Yusifs troops routed the Georgians and rounded up their commander. Ibrahim Khan was also taken prisoner. Many of Ibrahim's commanders and servicemen ended up as captives. This time Ibrahim Khan begged for his own life. He was pardoned. Later due to his charisma, education and tactfulness Qara Yusif made him Shirvan's ruler again.

The Last Days of Qara Yusif

Qara Yusif added Mosul and Mardin (1413) and other parts of Iraq (1416) to the vast possessions of Azerbaijan. On the eastern frontier of Azerbaijan, a new threat was looming. It was Tamerlane's son Shahrukh who longed for both his brother Miran's revenge (Miran was killed by the Azerbaijanis) and the fertile and rich lands of Azerbaijan. He declared war on Azerbaijan. Qara Yusif set out to meet him when he got sick and died in the city of Ujan. His army disintegrated[34].

Iskender Bey

Iskender bey took over the kingdom after his father Qara Yusif passed away. He drafted a new army in a very short time and marched to Baghdad. Later he clashed with Shahrukh's army at the lake Goyche (*also known today as Lake Sevan*). This was a long and bloody battle. Although Shahrukh's troops gained the upper hand towards the end of the skirmish they lost a catastrophic number of men. Shahrukh had no other choice but to withdraw his army from Azerbaijan. Iskender bey came back to Tabriz.

Iskender repulsed Shahrukh but faced another threat. His brother Abu Said made no secret of his plans to become the king of all Azerbaijan. They waged frequent wars against each other. Finally, a treaty was signed according to which Iskender would remain the king of historical Azerbaijan, while Abu Said would be the ruler of Iraq and other lands. But this peace did not last long. A new round of fighting began over the sovereignty over the city of Sultaniyye. Iskender took the city in 1428. Shahrukh was very upset about this move and sent his powerful army to help Abu Said. Iskender met Shahrukh in Selmas in Azerbaijan. Iskender suffered a defeat and had to retreat to East Anatolia (1430).

Shahrukh enthroned Abu Said as the king of Azerbaijan in Tabriz and went back to Khorasan. As soon as the news of Shahrukh's departure reached Iskender bey he rushed to Tabriz. On his way to Tabriz, he also fought and killed the Aghqoyunlu leader Qara Osman. Iskender entered Tabriz and vanquished Abu Said's forces executing Abu.

---

[34] Qara Yusif won the love of all the Chobanids when he was a shepherd (choban means a shepherd in Azerbaijani). The Chobanids swore by him. He always distributed the riches he gained to different tribes. No wonder that he was respected from Sham to Isfahan. He unified all of Azerbaijan, defeated Miran shah and fought two wars with Shahrukh. He died before the third one could start. He was the greatest of the Qaraqoyunlu rulers. Unfortunately, after his death his wealth was looted. Even his clothes were stolen. No one from his royal court even cared to bury him properly as his body lay on the central square for several days. Finally, common people arranged a decent burial.

After ridding himself of his two archenemies Iskender began contemplating a war against Shirvan. But Shirvan was an ally of the Tartars. At the same time, Shahrukh forged an alliance with the Aghqoyunlus and attacked Azerbaijan. Iskender was out of luck as his own wife and son became Tartar spies and conspired to kill him. Iskender saved his life by retreating to Erzurum in eastern Anatolia.

Iskender bey was a gifted general. He immediately reorganized his forces into highly mobile groups and began hitting the more powerful armies of his enemies in a guerrilla-style action. By the time Shahrukh's army reached Azerbaijan they found only corpses of their allies. Only the betrayal of his family and generals did prevent him from defending Azerbaijan further. Iskender had to retreat to Alinje fortress where he was murdered by his own son in 1437. Iskender bey was buried in Tabriz. He was a great and brave warrior and a wise statesman.

Jahanshah 1437-1467

Jahanshah had good relations with Shahrukh since it was the Tartars who helped him become the king. In 1440 he marched into Georgia. He occupied entire Georgia and brought it under the Azerbaijani control. In 1452 his army also annexed Iraq, Fars and Kerman. In 1456 Khorasan was destined to fall to Jahanshah. Then this Azerbaijani Shah expanded his possessions eastward. He defeated Alaud-Dovle ibn Baysungar at Jurjan and entered Herat. Jahanshah skirmished with Abu Said Khan, one of Tamerlane's grandsons. However, during this struggle Jahanshah's son Hasan Ali who had been imprisoned earlier escaped from the dungeon and began a mutiny in Tabriz. Jahanshah immediately signed a peace treaty with Abu Said and returned to the motherland. Hasan Ali was jailed again.

In another development, Jahanshah appointed another son, Pir Budag, the viceroy to Baghdad. Pir Budag had been ruling Fars before that promotion. But due to internal contradictions, Jahanshah sent an army to Baghdad and had Pir Budag hanged in 1465. After this action, Jahanshah stayed in Tabriz and focused on domestic affairs.

He was very active not only in expanding his territories but also in reforming the country. Jahanshah paid special attention to his capital city Tabriz. He ordered the construction of the famous "Goy Mechid" (Blue Mosque) in 1465. The ruins of that splendid mosque are still remaining in Tabriz.

The main reason for the demise of his rule was incessant attacks of the Aghqoyunlus. The protracted wars were draining the state's resources.

Finally, Jahanshah decided to go to an all-out war against the Aghqoyunlu chief Uzun (Tall) Hasan. It was the winter of 1467. Jahanshah ordered his army to the winter quarters to spend the winter there. Jahanshah and his son Mohammed Mirze were captured and killed as they fell behind their troops that and separated from them a great distance. Uzun Hasan had his other sons' eyes burned. Jahanshah's body was brought back to Tabriz and buried in "Blue Mosque".

Hasan Ali Padishah 1467-1468

Hasan Ali, Jahanshah's son took the throne in 1467. He had been condemned to prison in the Maku castle for 25 years. Because of this long imprisonment, he was not capable of running state affairs adequately. He warred with Uzun Hasan in 1467 and had to flee to Iran that was under the control of Abu Said. A year later he committed suicide as a result of deep depression. The Aghqoyunlus gradually removed all the Qaraqoyunlu sovereigns. Azerbaijan came under the rule of the Aghqoyunlus.

The Aghqoyunlus (Bayanduriyye)
The Aghqoyunlu Dynasty

We have already mentioned above that the Aghqoyunlu tribes settled in Mosul and Diyarbekir. Such great kings as Qara Osman, Hemz and Jahangir were Aghqoyunlu. The Aghqoyunlu king Uzun Hasan became the king of Azerbaijan. Here are some of the kings who descended from the Aghqoyunlu dynasty:

Bahaddin Qara Osman Gutlug ibn Turali (1406)
Jelaleddin Ali ibn Qara Osman (1434)
Nureddin Hemze ibn Qara Osman (1438)
Maghral ibn Jahangir ibn Ali (1444)
Uzun Hasan ibn Ali (1452)
Khalil ibn Hasan (1476)
Yagub ibn Hasan (1477)
Baysungar ibn Yagub (1490)
Rustam ibn Magsud ibn Hasan (1491)
Ahmed ibn Ughurlu Mohammed (1497)
Murad ibn Yagub (1497)
Mohammed ibn Yusif (1498)
Alvand Mirze ibn Yusif ibn Hasan (1500)
Zeynal ibn Ahmed ibn Ughurlu Mohammed (1504-1505)

Hasan ibn Yagub (1505-1508)
Murad ibn Yagub (second time) (1508)

Hasan Padishah (Better known as Uzun Hasan)

The Aghqoyunlu possessions were divided among the chieftains closest to Qara Osman after he had died in 1435. These small Khanates constantly fought each other for the sphere of influence. This chaos ended when Uzun Hasan from Qara Osman's family subjugated all of these principalities. He managed to restore the once-powerful state. Uzun Hasan demonstrated his strength in 1450 and 1456 during his campaigns against the Qaraqoyunlus in Azerbaijan. In 1467 he finally eradicated the Qaraqoyunlu dynasty after he had killed Jahanshah.

Meanwhile, Abu Said and other people loyal to Timur's family were planning to invade Azerbaijan. Abu Said entered the Azerbaijani city of Miyane in 1468. Uzun Hasan tried hard to resolve this conflict peacefully. But he failed as the Tartars invaded Karabakh. Uzun Hasan began a long and savage war against the aggressors. At last, he succeeded in exhausting Abu Said's troops so that Abu was forced to withdraw his forces from Azerbaijan. Uzun Hasan pursued the exhausted Tartar army and annihilated the remnants of Abu's troops killing Abu Said himself near Ardabil. The Khan of Shirvan was of great assistance in this war.

Abu Said was the last of the Tamerlaneids in Iran. The Aghqoyunlus added both Iraq and Fars to Azerbaijan's possessions becoming the only and absolute rulers in the region in 1468.

Uzun Hasan's Relations with the Ottomans

The relations between the Aghqoyunlus and the Ottomans were tense during Tamerlane's aggression. Their relations deteriorated even further as Uzun Hasan created an axis with small fiefdoms of Trabzon, Gastamoni and other places to fight the Ottomans. However, the Ottomans destroyed those small states in a short time and annexed them. They began an aggression against the Aghqoyunlus. The Ottomans acted freely close to the borders of Azerbaijan since Uzun Hasan was bogged down in the battles with the Qaraqoyunlus. Only after the victory over the Qaraqoyunlu dynasty could Uzun Hasan confront the Ottomans in an open battle.

Uzun Hasan allied himself with the ruler of Vand against the Ottomans. The first clashes occurred over the city of Greman. The two opposing warlords of Greman invited two different powers to assist them in their power struggle: one preferred the Ottomans while the other chose the Aghqoyunlus. The Ottoman Sultan Mehmet Fateh (*the Conqueror*) invaded Greman and liquidated any local political power. The former chieftains of Greman fled to Azerbaijan. In 1471 Uzun Hasan entered the area around Greman and stationed ten thousand troops there. Uzun Hasan himself, however, returned to Tabriz. Right after his return the Ottomans surrounded the 10,000 strong force to the west of Beksheher lake and defeated them. The following year Uzun Hasan attacked the Ottomans. Sultan Mehmet Fateh commanded his troops himself. The battle took place near a place called Terjan. The Sultan was victorious.

Uzun Hasan retreated to Azerbaijan. In 1475 he occupied Georgia, and the following year he passed away in Tabriz. The subsequent palace intrigues among his servicemen considerably weakened Azerbaijan.

Uzun Hasan was the greatest and most prominent of the Aghqoyunlus. He expanded the boundaries of Azerbaijan and ran the state very efficiently. He had seven sons: Ughurlu Mohammed, Magsud bey, Zeynal bey, Khalil bey, Sultan Yagub, Yusif Mirze and Masih Mirze. The first three sons died during Uzun Hasan's lifetime. Uzun Hasan was buried in a "Hasan Padishah" mosque in Tabriz. This mosque's construction was initiated by himself.

Sultan Khalil

After Uzun Hasan's death, his son Sultan Khalil became the emperor. Sultan had been the viceroy of the Fars region. He was inexperienced and soon alienated the powerful nobles in the palace. In 1477 his cousin Murad bey occupied Iraq. His control of Iraq did not last long as Sultan Khalil sent his army to crush the mutiny. Murad bey escaped to the Firuzguh castle where he was apprehended and brought to Tabriz. Later he was decapitated.

After many an internal conflict, the emirs persuaded Sultan Yagub, Sultan Khalil's brother, to claim the throne of Azerbaijan. Yagub was the sovereign in Diyarbekir at that time. A terrifying battle was fought by these two brothers in Marand. Sultan Khalil was killed in the fight and his rule in Azerbaijan ended.

Sultan Yagub

Sultan Yagub replaced his brother Sultan Khalil at the helm of power in 1477. The major political event under this king was the emergence of Sheikh Heydar in Ardabil. Sultan Yagub did not pay any attention to his movement as it was primarily a religious group. However, Shah Ismail who came from Heydar's family organized a strong army and defeated the Aghqoyunlus. He also spread Shiism in Azerbaijan in order to alienate the Azerbaijani Turks from their brethren in Anatolia (*see the publisher's note in Part 5*). This schism divided the Turkic world into two. That is why this event was the greatest political mistake of the Aghqoyunlus. If the matter had been handled in time it would not have resulted in the creation of a foreign power and weakening of Azerbaijan's Turkic government. This blunder dealt a serious blow to the whole Turkic world.

It is noteworthy that Sheikh Heydar asked Sultan Yagub's permission to travel to North Caucasus in order to proselytize Islam there. He was granted permission to pass through to the Caucasus. However, Sheikh gathered a sizable force and attacked Shirvan under the pretext of going to Derbend. The Khan of Shirvan was deeply worried about Heydar's plans. The Aghqoyunlus sent reinforcements to Shirvan at the Shirvan Khan's request. The Shirvan forces charged into Sheykh's armed groups and killed Sheikh.

After this battle supporters of Sheikh rose up several times demanding revenge for his death, but their uprising was suppressed, and Sheykh's close associates were arrested. In 1479 a certain warlord by the name of Bash bey stormed Diyarbekir, but the Azerbaijani army destroyed him within a few days. Sultan Yagub died in Karabakh in 1490. He was buried in the "Hasan Padishah" mosque in Tabriz. His mother Seljuk Shah Khatun and brother Yusuf Bey died when Yagub was still alive.

Baysungar Khan

Baysungar Khan was declared the king in 1490. Numerous wars and political upheavals happened under his rule. Below are the major events:

The war of Bayanduriyye. The death of Sultan Yagub caused the palace power struggle to intensify. One group of the statesmen supported Baysungar while the other camp backed his brother Masih Mirze. The Bayanduriyye tribe tried their best to enthrone Masih Mirze. Baysungar had to fight Mirze and the latter was defeated in Karabakh. Mirze was killed and his troops slaughtered. The supporters of Mirze who survived either escaped to Iraq or were imprisoned.

The Iraqi campaign. As we mentioned before some of Mirza's people fled to Iraq. Baysungar and Mirza's nephew Mahmud bey were among them. He recruited an army and decided to invade Azerbaijan. But

Baysungar acted faster and countered his forces in Iraq. Baysungar routed Mahmud's troops easily. Mahmud was captured when he attempted to escape and executed.

The betrayal of the Emirs. Besides the royal family, other political figures had their own ambitions regarding the throne of Azerbaijan. One of Baysungar's emirs, Sufi Khalil acquired substantial clout in the court. Baysungar entrusted him with practically all the state affairs. However, their relations deteriorated as Khalil's ambition reared its head. Sufi Khalil started undermining Baysungar Khan in order to install his friend Suleyman bey in Tabriz. Soon Suleyman bey stormed Tabriz, but his forces were rolled back. Sufi Khalil was executed for high treason. Baysungar Khan began looking after all the domestic affairs personally.

One of the enemies of Baysungar, Rustam bey was in the dungeon in Alinje Fortress. Some emirs plotted to get rid of Baysungar and after colluding with the ruler of Alinje Seyid Ali they set Rustam bey free. Rustam bey marched his troops against Baysungar Khan. Betrayed by his emirs Baysungar had to temporarily retreat to Shirvan. Rustam bey declared himself the king in Tabriz (1491).

Rustam Bey

Since taking the power in 1491 Rustam bey fought against Baysungar and Rustam's cousin Ahmed bey both of whom had claims to the throne.

The wars with Baysungar. After his forced retreat to Shirvan Baysungar Khan was plotting to assassinate the emirs who had betrayed him so that he could reclaim the crown in Tabriz. The two enemies clashed near Ganja and Barda several times. These battles were savage and bloody. Baysungar was bolstered by the Shirvan soldiers. However, no one could gain the upper hand in the fighting. They both pulled their armies from the area.

Then Baysungar joined forces with Kosa Haji Bayandur who was the chieftain in Isfahan and Baysungar's former viceroy. Their allied forces attacked Tabriz. They succeeded in occupying Mishkin and Ahar points in Azerbaijan. However, another enemy of Baysungar, Sheikh Heydar was waiting for his chance to revenge Baysungar in Ardabil. He gathered his men and attacked Baysungar killing him. Kosa Haji was murdered later that year.

Despite this event, the Safavids (Sheikh Heydar's supporters) rebelled against Rustam bey too. Rustam bey squashed this mutiny and killed their commander Ali Padishah. Young Ismail Safavid[35] managed to escape.

The conflict with Ahmed bey. Ahmed bey was given refuge in Anatolia by Sultan Bayazid. The Sultan demonstrated his respect for Ahmed bey by marrying his daughter to him and honoring him with the title of Pasha. Nevertheless, Ahmed bey never lost his hope of returning to Azerbaijan. He lived with a dream of taking the crown in Tabriz. His dreams came true when Sultan Bayazid agreed to send some Anatolian Seljuks and Turkmens under Ahmed bey's command to take Tabriz. Rustam bey met Ahmed bey at the Arax river. Rustam bey's emirs swapped the sides again causing Rustam's defeat. Rustam himself was caught and cut to death when he tried to escape to Georgia.

Ahmed Pasha

Rustam's cousin Ahmed Pasha came to power after Rustam had been murdered. His reign did not last long. Gasim bey, the mayor of Shiraz, joined Kerman's ruler Abya Sultan to attack Tabriz. They clashed near Isfahan. Ahmed Pasha fell in this fighting. Ahmed's cousin Murad Sultan was declared the king. Ahmed Pasha was a very wise statesman. He always paid exceptional attention to the well-being of his subjects. Ahmed Pasha is said to have had immense respect for poets and writers. His closest advisor was a philosopher by the name of Nogtechi oglu.

Sultan Murad

Sultan Murad, the son of Sultan Yagub ascended to the throne in 1497. His cousins fled the country in different directions. Mohammed Mirze, one of them, backed and instigated by the mayors of Yazd and Kerman fought against Sultan Murad. Sultan Murad defeated Mirza's forces near the city of Rey. Murad appointed his brother Gozel (handsome) Ahmed the sovereign in Rey and returned to Tabriz. Mohammed Mirze renewed his onslaught on Rey and forced Ahmed to flee. Mirze ran all the state affairs of Iraq and distinguished himself by performing this task efficiently. His popularity was increasing. Soon Mohammed Mirze invaded Tabriz with newly recruited troops. This time Sultan Murad was routed and forced to escape to Shiraz. Thus Mohammed Mirze triumphantly entered Tabriz.

---

[35] The future Azerbaijani Safavid Ruler known as Shah Ismail the First or Shah Ismail Khatai (The publisher's note).

Mohammed Mirze

In 1498 Mohammed Mirze was sworn in as the king. However, his other cousin Elvend Mirze had his own plans to take the crown. The latter was in the palace of Gasim bey, the mayor of Diyarbekir. Elvend Mirze took advantage of his close relations with Gasim bey and soon practically ruled the city. He was just waiting for an opportunity to invade Azerbaijan. Finally, he gathered a substantial army and besieged Tabriz. Mohammed Mirze suffered a defeat and had to flee to Sultaniyye. Elvend Mirze took Tabriz.

Elvend Mirze

During the rule of Elvend Mirze two of his cousins, Mohammed Mirze and Sultan Murad were plotting to seize the power. Thus, Mohammed Mirze formed an army from Iraq and Sultaniyye and moved against Isfahan where he was defeated by Murad. Mirze was jailed and his army dispersed except for a large force under his commander Pirali bey. Murad pursued Pirali bey and laid a siege to the Seva Fortress where Pirali bey decided to hold out. After fifty days of a siege, they signed a peace accord and agreed to fight Elvend Mirze together. Sultan Murad and Elvend Mirze met near the Sayin Fortress. However, thanks to the benevolence of a dervish by the name of Baba Kheyrulla, the conflict between these cousins was resolved by signing a peace treaty.

According to that treaty, Azerbaijan remained under Elvend Mirze while Iraq, Fars and Kerman went under the control of Sultan Murad. The Qizil Uzen river became the new border between their territories.

Sultan Murad tried to topple Gasim bey, the ruler of Shiraz, but was repulsed. This dual power continued until 1501 when Shah Ismail emerged on the political scene and eliminated these rulers. The same year the Aghqoyunlus were defeated at Sherur (in Nakhichevan region of the Republic of Azerbaijan) by the Safavids. This event was the turning point in the history of Azerbaijan as the Safavids seized the power.

Arts and Education in Azerbaijan under the Turkmen Dynasties

Two centuries after the rule of the Ilkhanids the arts and architecture made even more progress in Azerbaijan. The ruins of the Turkmen monuments in Tabriz are the living proof of that progress. Here are the major accomplishments of Azerbaijani architects of that era:

The Blue Mosque. This famous big mosque was erected by Jahanshah, the son of the great Aghqoyunlu leader Qara Yusif, in 1465. This Tabriz mosque is also known as the "Muzefferiyye" mosque. The ruins of this magnificent construction show the interior of the mosque that was replete with marble. The type and size of these marble stones still mesmerize the visitors. The flowery porcelain that decorates the mosque is incredibly exquisite. The pictures on these porcelain pieces were designed by joining pieces of different mold and color. The huge dome and two minarets were still intact until 1775 when a powerful earthquake leveled them. Only the walls of this great monument of the Turkic art do remain today. Jahanshah himself was buried in the Blue Mosque.

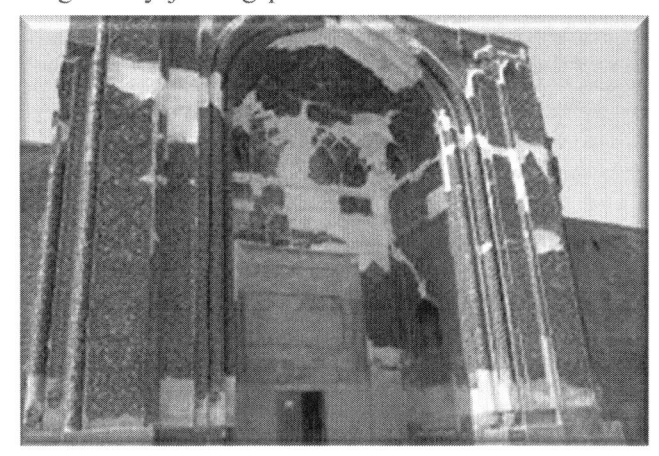

Blue Mosque, Tabriz, Capital of East Azerbaijan province, Iran

The Mosque of Hasan Padishah. The construction of this mosque was ordered by the Aghqoyunlu King Uzun Hasan. The original structure was damaged in the course of history. It was repaired and reconstructed in a plain and dull manner. Nevertheless, the original splendor was somewhat preserved since the Mosque's own pillars, carved stones, marbles and other elements were used during the repair works.

The following Aghqoyunlu kings were buried here: Uzun Hasan, Yagub Shah, Rustam Bey, Ahmed Pasha, Mohammed Bey and Baysungar Bey.

The fortress of Ark. The Ottoman Turks built this stronghold. It was first erected by Ibrahim Pasha during the reign of Sultan Salim Sani. But later it came into disrepair. Then in 1579, Ozdemir Osman Pasha undertook its reconstruction during the rule of Sultan Murad. Twin towers called "Ark" in Tabriz are the remnants of that fortress. The famous "Ali Shah" mosque was adjacent to this building.

Famous Azerbaijani poets such as Nasimi (1369-1417), Fizuli and others lived and created their literary masterpieces during this period. Fizuli was one of the first great poets to write his poems in Azerbaijani Turkish, and his works were published in Tabriz.

" I saw some scripts on your tall dais
Wonder what great times left them for us ..."?
      Mohammed Fizuli (1494-1556)

Fizuli Monument in central Baku, Azerbaijan Republic

PART FIVE

The Era of Independent Khanates (1501-1826)

Khanates of North Azerbaijan and South Azerbaijan
18th-19th century

Azerbaijan under the Ottoman Protection[36]

After the battle of Sherur, the Aghqoyunlu dynasty ended, and Azerbaijan came under the rule of Shah Ismail Safavid (*also known as Shah Ismail Khatai*). Such Aghqoyunlu chiefs as Sultan Murad, Elvend Mirze and others united their forces with Sultan Selim Khan of Anatolia against Shah Ismail. Shah Ismail managed to take over Azerbaijan. He united all the Turkmens who lived near Ardabil and Hamadan and went on an expansionist campaign. The former Azerbaijani kings were looking to Sultan Salim of the Ottoman Empire for help.

Sultan Salim was considered the great ruler of his time as his was also a vast empire in Europe. Sultan paid a special attention to the situation in brotherly Azerbaijan, and he was determined to save Azerbaijan from Persian and other non-Turkic influence. The latter were gaining ever more clout on the Azerbaijani soil. He undertook a major military effort and marched against the Safavid forces. In 1513 Sultan defeated the Safavid army at Chaldiran and forced Shah Ismail to retreat.

The statue of Shah Ismail I in Baku, Azerbaijan Republic

The following two centuries the Ottomans fought continuous wars to liberate Azerbaijan. There was no other conflict between the Turks and Persians but that problem. That is why the Persians interpreted the war as a sectarian one in order to separate the Azerbaijani Turks

---

[36] The author's position on the role of Shah Ismail the First in the Azerbaijani history is quite controversial and not shared by many Azerbaijani, Russian, Iranian and other historians. The modern Azerbaijani historiography considers Shah Ismail one of the greatest Azerbaijani rulers who united the Azerbaijani principalities under one powerful state. Shah Ismail was an Azerbaijani Turk who made the Azerbaijani language the state language of the Safavid Empire. He also wrote poetry in Azerbaijani under the penname of Khatai. His embrace of Shiism was considered a more political move to strengthen his power rather than an attempt to divide the Turkic world into two. Most Azerbaijani historians consider the Safavid-Ottoman wars a fratricidal conflict. (The publisher's note)

from their Ottoman brothers. The majority of the Iranian generals and soldiers were Azerbaijanis and Turkmens, in other words, Turks[37]. The Iranians incited the Azerbaijanis to seize the holy cities of Kerbela and Nejef thus further fueling the religious sentiments. Let us describe the major wars between the Ottomans and Iran during those two centuries.

Sultan Salim Khan the First

The Chaldiran Battle. In 1513 the Ottoman army under the command of Sultan Salim faced the Iranian army near the village of Chaldiran to the west of the city of Khoy. After the repeated peace appeals of the Ottomans, the Iranians answered with hostilities. A large-scale battle took place in Chaldiran. The Iranians were routed, and Shah Ismail fled. Consequently, all Azerbaijan came under the control of the Ottomans. The Azerbaijanis fought alongside the Ottoman army in this war. Burhan Eli, the Khan of Shirvan, took over Shirvan with his small armed group. The Ottoman army moved back to Erzurum to spend the winter. The Iranians reoccupied Azerbaijan again.

Sultan Suleyman the Lawful

Sultan Suleyman replaced Sultan Salim and undertook three military campaigns against Iran.

The Baghdad campaign. In 1534 Sultan Suleyman liberated Azerbaijan from the Iranians and occupied Baghdad. This operation lasted six months after which Suleyman returned to Anatolia.

The Tabriz campaign. On the departure of the Turkish troops, the Iranians invaded Azerbaijan again. Sultan Suleyman in response to this aggression stormed Tabriz and seized Azerbaijan and Georgia.

Although the Iranians attempted to attack Azerbaijan Sultan Suleyman instigated the Iranian fratricide by supporting Elgas Mirze, the brother of the Iranian Shah Tehmasib.

The Azerbaijanis made cities of Ganja, then Shemakha their capitals at different periods of their history. They now declared Tabriz the capital city. Tabriz found prosperity under an Azerbaijani dynasty of the Atabegs.

---

[37] The author did not cover almost 400 years of the Azerbaijani history in the southern part of Azerbaijan, which is now part of Iran. This history included great Azerbaijani Turkic ruling dynasties such as the Safavids, Afsharids and Qajars. He does not give any explanation but perhaps his antipathy towards the Safavids could be the reason. (The publisher's note).

Tabriz. The city was destroyed during Genghis Khan's invasion. However, it was rebuilt by the Ilkhanids. Tabriz was converted into their center again. Gazan Khan was the ruler who spent a large part of his treasury to beautify the city by ordering the construction of Rashidiyye and Shami Gazan castles. Tamerlane the Lame was believed to take care of the city as well. Such beautiful mosques as Hasan Padishah and Blue Mosque were erected under the Turkmens.

Regrettably, the frequent earthquakes ruined the once magnificent architecture of Tabriz. Then the Iran-Ottoman wars took a serious toll on the city's buildings. Finally, after the Persian occupation of Tabriz it completely lost its importance and its infrastructure came into decay. The earthquakes of 1722 and 1775 resulted in a colossal loss of life.

Tabriz gave birth to many poets and scientists as it was a historically important and large metropolis. Although most of these poets have been "serving" the Persian language their native Azerbaijani Turkish was not completely forgotten either. The following two lines are the way the Tabrizis praised their homeland:

"In the past glittering Shiraz was the latest word,
But today Tabriz is the capital of the world."

The Nakhichevan Campaign. The Iranians were pushing forward with their onslaught. Even Ehlat and Erzurum were occupied. Sultan Suleyman himself led his troops against the enemy and entered Nakhichevan. The Iranians retreated without any resistance. The Ottomans stayed in Karabakh to spend the winter. The two sides signed a peace treaty. According to this document Azerbaijan which had changed hands for forty-two years remained under the Iranian occupation.

Sultan Murad Khan the Third

Peace with Iran did not last long, and a war broke out again. This conflict lasted twelve years. Here are the major military engagements.

The Offensive by Lala Mustafa Pasha. In 1577 Mustafa Pasha conquered Georgia, Sheki, Shirvan and Derbend. He organized the state apparatus in Azerbaijan and returned to Anatolia. Immediately on his return, the Iranians besieged Tiflis (Tbilisi) and threatened Baghdad and Erzurum.

The Campaign by Senan Pasha. Senan Pasha was appointed a new commander of the Iranian front. He broke the siege of Tiflis and in his turn besieged Tabriz. At the same time, another Ottoman general by the name of Ozdemir Osman Pasha defeated the Iranians at the banks of the Samur River and captured Azerbaijan all the way to the Caucasian Mountains. Ozdemir withdrew with his forces through Daghestan and Crimea.

The Campaign by Ozdemir Osman Pasha. Ozdemir launched another offensive against the Iranian army. His army captured Tabriz. But after the defeat at the Shami Gazan fortress, Osman Pasha died of the grief. He spared no effort to help erect new buildings and restore the old ones in Azerbaijan. Even today one can see the glorious twin towers known as Ark in Tabriz. Osman Pasha had them built in 1579. Jighalzade took over after Osman's death.

Ferhat Pasha's Offensives. Ferhat Pasha became a new commander to fight Iran. Tabriz was under a siege, and Tiflis' security was also threatened. Ferhat Pasha won over the Turkmens who fought in the Iranian army and saved Tiflis. Jighalzade on the other hand conquered Hamadan and Loristan and defeated Iranians near Baghdad. Within a short period, Ferhat Pasha occupied entire Azerbaijan. In the end, he signed a peace accord with Shah Abbas under the terms of which Azerbaijan, Georgia, Loristan and Shehrzur stayed within the Ottoman influence.

Sultan Ahmed the First

The war broke out again. Shah Abbas incited by the Pope in Europe and the Selmas Kurds in Azerbaijan violated the cease-fire and suddenly invaded Azerbaijan. He defeated the Azerbaijani forces in Sufiyan. Unfortunately, the Jelalid rebellion in Anatolia did not let the Ottomans defend Azerbaijan from the Iranian aggression. Under such favorable conditions for the Iranians, Shah Abbas seized Tabriz and Nakhichevan and laid a siege to Irevan (*today it more commonly known as Yerevan*). Shah Abbas occupied Irevan after six months. His army looted Kars, Shirvan and Shikhli and massacred the civilians. Jighalzade made an unsuccessful attempt to help Azerbaijanis. Only after having suppressed the rebellion in Anatolia could Ferhat Pasha liberate Azerbaijan. At last, the Ottomans and Shah Abbas signed a new peace agreement that outlined the demarcation zones that had been determined by Sultan Suleyman the Lawful. The Iranians were obliged by the treaty to deliver 200 camel loads of silk every year as a tribute.

Sultan Osman the Second

200 camel loads of silk were the annual tax levied from Azerbaijan. Although Azerbaijan remained under the Iranian rule the Persians were supposed to collect the silk and transport it to Turkey. The Iranians refused

to pay this tribute, and the Ottomans attacked Iran. Their troops reached Iran through Irevan-Nakhichevan and occupied Azerbaijan. On their way back the Ottomans stayed in Erzurum to spend the winter. However, many Ottoman soldiers died in the Soghanlig pass because of unusually cold winter.

The Crimean Tartars were a great help in this war. Their leader Janibey Geray entered Azerbaijan via the North Caucasus and ousted Iranians from Ganja, Nakhichevan and Julfa. Then he joined his forces with the Ottomans in capturing Tabriz. However, Janibey launched a single-handed attack on the Iranians in Serab and was defeated. He escaped the death although most of his Tartar emirs fell in this battle. Later that year Khalil Pasha himself moved towards Ardabil, and the Iranians retreated.

Finally, in 1617, a peace accord was signed again according to which 200 camel loads of silk and 100 loads of other valuables were to be paid by the Iranians in war reparations. Two years later the Iranian envoy Gasim bey arrived in Istanbul with precious gifts and expanded this peace treaty by allowing the Ottomans to control Baghdad and Akhsekhe. Hevize, Mughan, Shamkhal and Daghestan were to remain independent.

The Division of Azerbaijan
Iranian Azerbaijan

The year 1619 will be remembered by us, the Turks, forever as the most tragic moment in the history of our nation. In that auspicious year after 100 years of ruthless wars, Southern Azerbaijan was officially given to Iran. Since there was no natural boundary between Tehran and the river Arax, Tabriz and all the surrounding areas came under the Iranian dominance, while Shirvan and Mughan to the north of the Arax were left as independent states.

In 1619 Azerbaijan was divided into two parts now known as Iranian Azerbaijan and Caucasian Azerbaijan. This division was intact until the Russian occupation of Caucasian or North Azerbaijan. Today, to our ultimate dismay, most Azerbaijanis in Iran have been Persified[38], and they are just a province under the Persian yoke.

---

[38] The author makes an exaggeration by claiming that the Azerbaijani population of Tabriz, Ardebil and other large cities of Southern Azerbaijan had been Persified. Today there are many millions of Azerbaijanis in those and other cities of Southern Azerbaijan and Iran who speak Azerbaijani as their mother tongue. Nevertheless, the author is correct in pointing out the discrimination of Azerbaijanis in Iran. For example, there are no Azerbaijani-language schools in Southern Azerbaijan even today although the Azerbaijanis account for 30-40% of Iran's population. (The publisher's note)

The Azerbaijanis in the Caucasus, however, as we are going to bring to your attention, did not cave in to innumerable pressures and aggressions. They preserved their Turkishness and created an independent Turkic Azerbaijani state. But we should emphasize that only the people living in Tabriz, Ardabil and other cities have been Persified. In other parts of Azerbaijan, the population do not even know the language of the Persians. Especially such Azerbaijani tribes as the Karabakh, Ardabil and Mishkin shahsevens and others do not succumb to the pressures and assimilation attempts of the Iranian authorities.

The Iranian Turks - they are the most active, the most valuable part of Iran's people comprising two-thirds of the population. But their situation in Iran is very poor and tragic. The Persians and other foreign groups constantly insult them by calling them "turka kherend". And the Ottomans call these Turks foreigners without distinguishing them from the Persians. These unfortunate Turks themselves do not know properly who they are.

Although the Turks have settled in Iran centuries ago and already mastered Iranian language, their culture and traditions, the Persians still consider them a hostile and unfriendly group. The Persians harbor the same animosity to them as they did to the ancient tribes of Turan in the past.

Even until recently (30-40 years ago) the Persians were organizing pogroms of the Turks in Meshhed, the center of Khorasan province. The bandits were breaking into the houses of the Turkish families and asking them to say the word "gusht" (meat in Persian), if the innocent people said "gtisht" with the Turkish accent they were massacred on the spot.

The situation in Iranian Azerbaijan is even more tragic. Here even the very existence of the national consciousness and identity is jeopardized. The Azerbaijanis are prohibited from using their native tongue in schools, media and books. Anyone attempting to do so is severely persecuted. Today there are no books published in Azerbaijani Turkish in Iranian Azerbaijan with the exception of religious books. There are a great number of Turkish-language books on religion all over Azerbaijan. In order to promote their own religious and political ends, the Iranian authorities inundate even the most remote Azerbaijani villages with religious publications in our mother tongue.

Such is the tragic policy of the Tehran government towards Iranian Azerbaijan. In other words, the Persians are carrying out such terrible assimilation and persecution programs that even the Russian Czars did not attempt to implement in Caucasian Azerbaijan. However, the Shahs in Tehran are going to get what the Czars in Russia have already gotten. Just like the Azerbaijanis began their national liberation movement during the revolution in Iran, their Turkic self-awareness will awaken again at the first opportunity.

The Shahsevens (literally those who love Shah)

Yunis Pasha migrated from Anatolia to Iran with three thousand tents and settled in Azerbaijan and primarily around Ardabil. This movement happened during the reign of Shah Abbas, and the reasons behind this massive migration are not known. Yunis Pasha had the following offspring Sarukhan bey, Polad bey and Khoja bey. Qurd bey, Yunis' close friend, was supported by the nobles by the names of Polad bey, Demirchali and Guzat bey. The tribes that originated from these people were named after themselves. Although there were 32 tribes of Shahsevens, it is believed that the original number of the groups was larger.

Bedirkhan, one of Yunis Pasha's grandsons, became extremely popular under the rule of Nadir Shah. However, after his death, his first generals Kichik khan and Nezereli khan began a power struggle which led to the division of the Shahsevens into two groups. Kichik Khan's supporters made the city of Mishkin and its suburbs their home, while the followers of Nezereli Khan chose Ardabil for their permanent settlement.

The Tribes of Mishkin are -Mestelibeyli, Qara Gasimli, Novruzelibeyli, Serukhanbeyli, Talish Mikayil, Jayizli, Ivdili, Muradli Shahverdi bey, Seyidan, Mughanli, Demirchali, Arabli, Milli, Balabeyli, Murad Shahbazali bey, Khojabeyli Isa bey, Khelfeli, Zerger, Chalvadarli, Beybaghli, Charyarli, Beydili, Gamunlu, Berayuatli, Khojakhojali, Kekilli, Kor Abbasli, Hussein Khojali, Gapadli, Kilash, Ajirli, Yeddi Oyman, Shahelibeyli, Sari Jeferli, Saribanan, Ilkhichi, Khojabeyli Nurulla bey, Shikhalibeyli, Hajivelili, Kebedli, Eynalli, Gulushchu, Gehre manbeyli.

The Ardabil Shahsevens. The following were the tribes of Ardabil Shahsevens: Asifeli Khamuslu, Churukhlu, Rzabeyli, Tekle, Jahankhanimli, Eskeli, Beybulagli, Guzatli, Yurtchu, Dursunkhojali, Poladli, Shikhli, Ferejullahkhanli and Abibeyli.

These tribes have always served the Iranian shahs loyally. Since they were the only stable and strong support of the Iranian Shahs they came to be known as Shahsevens or those who love shah. Their language was Western Turkic (Ottoman and Azerbaijani). The Zerger tribe was the only group that spoke Chighatay dialect of the Turkic.

The Shahsevens' administration was run by the chief called "Elbeyi" (literally from Azerbaijani "the chief or noble of the tribe/land"). Besides the tribute of 12 thousand tumens to the Iranian Shah, they had complete independence. The tribes, however, were constantly involved in internal strife. The wars between them were quite frequent. So, these are the famous Shahsevens whom the Iranian Shahs respected and feared. In 1907, the Russian Emperor declared a war on the Shahsevens at the request of the Iranian Shah. The Shahsevens were defeated only because of their inability to put their internal disputes aside and unite their forces against the enemy.

These Turkic tribes lack educational facilities today. The Tehran government has done its best to keep these Turks in the darkness of illiteracy. That is why it is important to establish a system that would meet all the needs of these warlike and brave Turkic tribes and create conditions when these Turks would serve their motherland efficiently.

Sultan Murad the Fourth

Under this Ottoman Sultan, the Iranians captured Baghdad and Georgia. Sultan Murad himself marched into Azerbaijan and occupied Irevan and Tabriz. He returned to Istanbul before winter. The Iranians, consequently, seized Akhsikhe, Irevan, Kerkuk and Sherur.

In 1636, the Iranians sent a diplomat by the name of Gasim bey to Istanbul to negotiate a peace treaty. However, the talks went wrong, and Gasim bey was thrown in jail. The war continued. In 1637, Sultan Murad took Baghdad after forty days of a siege. Finally, the warring sides signed a peace accord under which Azerbaijan remained in the Iranian sphere of influence, while Baghdad, Kars and Akhsikhe were controlled by the Ottomans.

Sultan Ahmed the Third

In 1711, on his return from a pilgrimage to Mecca, Haji Davud (one of the Azerbaijani generals) together with the Daghestani Khan Surkhay Khan set off a mutiny in order to expel the Iranians from Azerbaijan. They succeeded in Shemakha where they ousted the Iranian administration and confiscated the merchandise that belonged to Russian and Persian traders.

However, overall, the operation failed. In 1715, when Iran was invaded by the Afghan warriors, Haji Davud and Surkhay khan attacked the Iranians again. They drove the Iranians out of Shirvan completely and surrounded Derbend. As the mayor of Derbend fled to Isfahan all of North Azerbaijan was finally liberated from the Iranian occupation.

Although the country was freed from the aggressor from the South, even a bigger threat was looming in the North. The Russians were contemplating an invasion into Azerbaijan. It was that time Peter the First occupied the Iranian coastline taking advantage of the power struggle among the Iranians. After the death of Shah Hussein his sons Tehmasib and Mir Ashraf were squabbling with each other for the throne.

The Russians attempted to invade Azerbaijan under the pretext of defending the interests of the Russian merchants who had suffered at the hands of Azerbaijanis. Haji Davud traveled to Istanbul to seek help from the only hope of Azerbaijanis and all Turks, that is the Ottoman ruler. The Ottomans announced their readiness to defend Azerbaijan and appointed Davud the viceroy in Shirvan. This, however, caused friction between Davud and Surkhay khan who also yearned for an exalted position. After short skirmishes between the two, Surkhay became the sovereign of Shirvan while Davud was appointed the ruler of Ganja.

Meanwhile, the Ottomans moved their army to Azerbaijan to liberate it from the Russian aggressors. The Turkish Army took over Georgia, Shirvan and Mughan. Peter the First appealed to France to settle the conflict peacefully. Under the French pressure Daghestan, Derbend and Baku were given to Russia, while the rest of Azerbaijan went under Ottoman protection.

However, the population in Istanbul was outraged and took to the streets with the slogan "The Turks were betrayed to the Muscovites". The situation was exacerbated further by a renewed attempt by Iran to invade Azerbaijan.

Ibrahim Pasha entered Azerbaijan and captured the cities of Tabriz and Irevan. Another Ottoman army under the command of Ahmed Pasha routed Shah Tehmasib and occupied Hamadan. Ahmed Pasha pursued the fleeing Iranian troops. Shah Tehmasib had no other choice but to sue for peace. The two sides agreed that South Azerbaijan would remain under the rule of Tehran while North Azerbaijan, Daghestan and Georgia would go to the Ottomans. However, at that time a general by the name of Nadir revolted against Shah Tehmasib and succeeded in toppling him. Nadir brought Shah Tehmasib's son Abbas Mirze to power. At the same time, Nadir declared war against the Ottomans and was heartily supported by the Russian Empire and the Armenian armed gangs[39].

---

[39] For example, in Ganja the forces of Sari Mustafa Pasha were attacked at night and were practically destroyed. Sari Mustafa Pasha had to retreat with the remnants of his army to Irevan. This sudden attack was the work of an Armenian by the name of Melik Avanan.

Meanwhile, the Crimean Khan Feth Geray Khan gathered his troops and entered Azerbaijan in order to help the cornered Azerbaijanis. His effort failed. Nadir occupied Ganja and Irevan and returned to Isfahan to be enthroned as the Shah of Iran. After that event, he also signed a peace treaty with the Ottomans according to which Azerbaijan together with Georgia went under the Iranian rule.

The second mobilization. Nadir Shah appointed his brother Ibrahim Khan the viceroy in Azerbaijan and marched to the east of Iran to fight the Afghans. The Azerbaijani people revolted against the Iranian oppression and overthrew the Iranian appointee in Derbend. The Azerbaijani Lezghins attacked Shemakha, defeated the Iranian forces and killed Ibrahim Khan. Nadir Khan launched a punitive expedition in order to revenge his brother's death. He moved a large army against Azerbaijan and captured the cities of Quba and Shemakha. Nadir also succeeded in arresting 84 generals and high-ranking officials from Daghestan who later managed to escape.

Nadir Shah continued his march through Daghestan and reached the borders of Russia. The two sides began making preparations for a major war over the status of the city of Gizlar ("girls" literally from Azerbaijani) in North Caucasus. But the domestic affairs in Iran were deteriorating, so Nadir had to return to his capital. Nadir Shah stationed his troops in Azerbaijan and Daghestan for two years. There was absolutely no impact of the Iranians on the lives of the two countries within those two years. Nadir went back. On his way back home, his army suffered great losses because of the severe conditions they were in. It is believed that half of his one-hundred-thousand-strong army perished in this march. Thus, Nadir returned to Gazvin through Mughan. Nadir Shah was assassinated in Khorasan and was buried in Meshhed. Iranians did not take care of his grave for a long time. Only later did the common people erect a shrine for Nadir Shah in the Bala Khiyaban neighborhood of the city. A new garden that was worth Nadir's name was also created near his shrine.

The Independent Khanates in Azerbaijan

We have already mentioned above that South Azerbaijan remained under Iranian rule as a province. The Northern part of the country was ruled by different Khanates that had been small principalities before too.

Nadir Shah honored Melik with great titles and gifts. After Melik's emigration to Russia, he was honored the same way by the Russian Emperor. On the occasion of that "holiday" (the massacre of the Turks in Ganja), the Russian Emperor sent his congratulations to Nadir Shah.

Some new Khanates also emerged during that period. We will briefly discuss the major Khanates and Emirates below.

Shirvan

There were two main routes that were connecting the northern and southern parts of the Caucasus from the beginning of time. One of them was the road traversing through Derbend. The ancient Greeks called these gates the "Caspian Gates". The other one was the route going via Vladigafgas that was known as Deryal[40]. The mass influx of the Khazars into Azerbaijan was proceeding through Derbend. The Derbend Fortress was built for the purpose of stopping the incursion of the Khazars. However, the Derbend Fortress alone could not prevent the Khazars from populating Azerbaijan. That is why the "Shirvan", "Anji[41]" and other fortresses were constructed.

Shirvan borders Georgia in the west, the Caucasian Mountains in the north, the Kura River in the south, and its eastern coast is washed by the Caspian Sea. Although Shirvan was part of Azerbaijan, the local lords were practically independent. At some point, these sovereigns even had the title of Shirvan Shahs.

The Shirvanshahs

The First Dynasty. The local rulers of Shirvan were Zoroastrians before the Arab invasion. After the Islamization in Azerbaijan, the Arabs appointed their own emirs as viceroys in Shirvan. However, there is little information as to how these people ran the government. The only known fact is that the founder of the dynasty Surkhab was a son of the Iranian Shah Jamasp.

The local Emirs declared their independence after the demise of the Arab Empire. In 790 Yezid ib Mezid ibn Sheybani took over the state administration in Shirvan. His descendants continued to run the government after his death.

---

[40] Deryal- means deren-alan that is the valley of the Alans (dere means valley in Azerbaijani). The valley was named after the Alan tribes who used to settle in valleys.

[41] Anji - the Russians call it Petrovski nowadays. It is a lovely port town situated on the western coast of the Caspian Sea. This town became to be known as Unji ("un" means flour in Azerbaijani), then Anji, as it used to be an important junction for the transportation of the flour.

The Second Dynasty. The Mezyeddids. The second Arab dynasty was called Mezyeddids. Ibn Sheybani was appointed the viceroy to Shejistan in 768. Then he went to Ehlat as an Emir. Finally, after having been summoned back to the Caliphate he was reappointed as the viceroy of Azerbaijan in 789. He died in 801 and was buried in Barda.

His administrators founded the first Muslim dynasty in Shirvan. This dynasty is believed to have ruled Shirvan till 1048. The third dynasty replaced the Mezyeddids.

The Shirvanshahs Palace Complex, Baku, Azerbaijan

The Third Dynasty. The Kesranids. The Kesranid Dynasty was founded by a certain Feriberz. His origins or nationality are not known to us today. However, the coins that have survived to our times give us a clue regarding the names of the rulers who have originated from this dynasty.

1. Melik Feriberz (1048)
2. Manuchehr ibn Feriberz the First (1106)
3. Ehsitan ibn Manuchehr (1149)
4. Feriberz ibn Firidun the Second (1194)
5. Ferrokhzad ibn Manuchehr (1203)
6. Kershasp ibn Ferrokhzad (1214)
7. Feriberz ibn Kershasp the Third (1225)
8. Ehsitan ibn Feriberz (1248)
9. Ferrokhzad ibn Ehsitan the Second (1258)
10. Keygubad (1284)
11. Kavus ibn Keygubad (1345)
12. Husheng ibn Kavus (1372-1378)

After the end of the Kesranid Dynasty and the long power vacuum, the local Derbendi dynasty came to power.

The Fourth Dynasty. The Derbendis. The common people were tired and worn out by endless feuds between local warlords. Finally, the people installed Sheikh Ibrahim ibn Mohammed Derbendi as their shah. Below are the rulers from the Derbendi Dynasty:

1. Sheikh Ibrahim ibn Mohammed Derbendi (1382)
2. Khelilullah ibn Ibrahim the First (1416)
3. Hasan bey Farrukh Yasar (1462)
4. Behram bey ibn Farrukh Yasar (1500)
5. Gazi bey ibn Farrukh Yasar (1501)
6. Sultan Mahmud ibn Gazi bey (1502)
7. Sheikh lbrahim ibn Gazi bey the Second (1502)
8. Khelilullah ibn Ibrahim the Second (1523)
9. Shahrukh ibn Ferej Mirze ibn Ibrahim (1535)
10. Burhan Eli ibn Khelilullah the Second (1537-1549)

These khans lived in peace as part of Azerbaijan. However, after the occupation of Azerbaijan by the Russians and Iranians, these Khanates were systematically invaded and looted by the northern and southern aggressors.

Burhan Eli Khan supported the Aghqoyunlus against the Ottomans on the eve of the division of Azerbaijan. He was defeated and forced to flee to Daghestan where he later died. Burhan Eli's son Abubekr Mirze participated in the military campaigns of Sultan Selim khan and Sultan Suleyman the Lawful. He died in Shemakha, the capital of Shirvan in 1549. His death marked the demise of the Derbendi dynasty.

The New Khanates

The new Khanates emerged on the territory of Shirvan. Those were Baku Khanate, Quba Khanate, Derbend Khanate, Sheki Khanate, Jarbelakan Khanate and Ilisu Khanate.

The centers of these Khanates carried the same name as the Khanates themselves. The last two Khanates were called Jarbelakan and Ilisu after the branches of the Gapichay river that forked in the area the Russians called Zagatal.

Mughan

The lands between the Arax and Kura rivers in Azerbaijan are known as Mughan. Mughan borders Georgia in the West and is washed by the Caspian Sea in the east. The city of Barda used to be the capital of Mughan. This area of Azerbaijan has been highly developed since ancient times. As its population grew other large cities were founded as well.

Ganja - existed even before the time of Alexander the Great. As it was the junction point of many roads Ganja became an important commercial city. The present-day Ganja is situated seven kilometers to the south of the ancient city of Ganja.

Hemishre- is believed to have been founded by an Iranian sovereign named Abrshehri. It came into decay and lost its importance later in history. Today there is a village in Mughan with the same name. It is famous for its weekly fairs.

Bilesuvar - was built by Emir Bilesuvar in 933-958. A village of the same name still exists in Azerbaijan.

Bajrevan - used to be a large city in Mughan. However, no ruins of that city can be found today.

Mahmudabad - was founded by the Azerbaijani Ilkhan Gazan Mahmud khan in 1295-1352. No remnants of the city survived to our day.

Beylagan - was a sizable city to the south of Barda. Genghis Khan's invasions considerably damaged the city, but later Tamerlane reconstructed Beylegan. There are no remnants of Beylegan either[42].

The Mughan Khanates
Karabakh Khanate
Penah Khan

Penah Khan established the Karabakh Khanate in 1749. It was then that Nadir Shah was exiling many Azerbaijani tribes from Mughan to Khorasan in Iran. The tribe called the Javanshirs with its leader Ali bey Sarijali also known among the people as Penah Khan was one of the exiled.

Later Penah khan returned to his country and created an independent Khanate called Karabakh Khanate with its capital in Penahabad, today's city

---

[42] The ruins of the ancient Beylagan are about 22 km from the modern city of Beylegan in the Azerbaijan Republic (The publisher's note).

of Shusha[43]. Penah khan was a very wise and capable state figure. The Khanate made significant strides in many areas under his rule.

The following are the principal political events that occurred under the rule of Penah Khan.

The Georgia campaigns. In 1749, after Nadir Shah's retreat to Iran, Penah Khan decided to revenge the Georgians for the assistance they had provided to the Iranians. He concluded a pact with the neighboring Ganja, Sheki, Shirvan and Jarbelakan Khanates and attacked Georgia. However, in the battles that occurred near the villages of Margubi and Didopisiali, Penah Khan's forces were defeated by the Georgian King Irakli.

The Khan of Irevan was also helping Irakli in this confrontation. Penah khan took advantage of the political unrest in Ganja, which was his ally, and captured the city. But the Armenians in Ganja asked the Georgian King for assistance. And the Georgian Prince Teymur under the pretext of obtaining the unpaid tribute of Ganja defeated Penah Khan again.

After this war, Prince Teymur returned to Ganja which was flooded by the belligerent Shahsevens from Southern Azerbaijan. Teymur defeated them and embarked on pursuing the Shahsevens all the way to Barda. However, the Khan of Sheki completely routed the Georgian forces near Jar.

The new khan of Ganja Shahverdi Khan refused to pay annual taxes to Teymur who invaded Ganja again. The Georgians backed by the Irevan and Sheki khans were victorious in this war.

Later that year Ganja, Shirvan, Derbend and Jar Khans united their forces and moved against the Georgians. They stationed their troops in Qazakh and Shemseddin for too long. Meanwhile, Teymur hired Kabardins, Ossetians and other people from North Caucasus for thirty manats a month to fight on his side. Teymur won this battle. The Sheki khan together with his allies had to return to Sheki. Thus, the Georgian affairs were left halfway.

The Mutiny of Afghans. In 1751 an Afghan soldier by the name of Azadkhan gathered the Afghans and Uzbeks and attempted to seize the power in Azerbaijan. The Afghans came to Azerbaijan during the Iranian invasion.

Although they succeeded in capturing Tabriz, Urmiyye, Khoy and Selmas, their siege of Irevan was broken by the Georgians, the allies of Iran. The Iranians sent a certain Mohammed Hasan Khan Qajarli to Azerbaijan to organize a movement against the Afghans. This person

---

[43] Shusha is currently under the Armenian military occupation in Nagorno Karabakh of Azerbaijan Republic (The publisher's note)

could secure no help from the local feudal lords. The Lenkoran Khan Qarakhan drove Qajarli's forces out of Azerbaijan. Then the latter laid a siege to the city of Shusha in Karabakh and asked Georgia for help. He was defeated again. Qajarli finally had to return to Iran after Kerimkhan Zend began a rebellion in Iran. On his way back he was attacked and beaten by Karabakh and Sheki khans.

The Rebellion of the Afshars. **An** Afshari named Fetheli Khan from the Iranian ruling circles began a mutiny. He occupied Tabriz, and his troops surrounded Shusha. Nevertheless, even very active help from the Georgians did not facilitate his siege effort. Fetheli Khan had to withdraw to Tabriz. His troops accidentally stumbled into Kerimkhan Zend's forces and were thoroughly defeated. The rebellion was crushed.

Ibrahim Khan

After Penah Khan's death, his son Ibrahim took over the state matters. He expanded the territories of the Khanate and fortified its capital city of Shusha. Ibrahim Khan established very friendly relations with the Georgian King Irakli. However, during his reign, the Karabakh Khanate faced new threats.

The Invasion by Agha Mohammed Shah Qajar[44]

The Azerbaijani Khans did not recognize the legitimacy of Agha Mohammed Shah Qajar's rule in Iran right from the beginning. Qajar in his turn marched against Azerbaijan in order to subjugate the Khanates. He dispatched his brother Aligulu Khan to seize Irevan, and himself crossed the Arax river through the Khudaferin bridge and laid siege to Shusha. However, the siege dragged on, and the Shah's efforts to breach the city walls failed. The Georgians who did not recognize the Shah also supported the Azerbaijani Khanate.

Qajar changed his plans and now was determined to subdue Georgia before trying to capture Shusha. Meanwhile, his brother Aligulu Khan occupied Irevan and exiled its khan Mohammed Khan to Tehran together with his family.

Under such favorable conditions, Qajar Shah launched an offensive against Georgia jointly with his brother. Jefergulu Khan, the khan of Khoy, Kelbeli Khan, the khan of Nakhichevan and Javad Khan of Ganja sent their troops to help Qajar in this war.

---

[44] The Qajar dynasty were of Azerbaijani Turkic descent as well originating from Qoyunlu branch of the Qajars (The publisher's note)

The forces of the Georgian King Irakli the Second defended the city walls against the Shah's onslaughts. But the forces were far from being equal, and the Georgians were forced to flee the city in the direction of Dushet. The Iranians entered Tiflis on October 12th and left the city after twenty-five days.

The following year Qajar attacked Azerbaijan again. After ferocious fighting, he reached the city walls of Shusha. The city was surrounded. The conditions of the troops of Ibrahim Khan were deteriorating rapidly. The Shah sent a letter to the Khan with the following words: "Are you hoping to defend yourself in a glass jar when the rocks are raining from the sky?"

The response of the great Azerbaijani poet Vagif (the native of Shusha, and the vizier of the Khan) to this challenge was as heroic and proud as the defenders of the city: "The Almighty God who protects me will also preserve the glass under the avalanche of rocks."

Nevertheless, a handful of Azerbaijani fighters could not hold out against tens of thousands of Iranian troops. The Khan had to retreat to Jarbelakan. Qajar Shah broke into Shusha but was immediately assassinated[45]. His army was forced to withdraw from Karabakh to Iran. Later that year Ibrahim Khan returned to his country.

The new Iranian Shah Fetheli Shah signed a peace accord with Ibrahim Khan. Fetheli Shah married Ibrahim's daughter Beyim khanim. She was the main figure in the harem of the Shah. In that year, the British Queen sent a precious gift to the Iranian Royal Court. That gift was handed to Beyim khanim who in return sent a letter thanking the English Queen for the valuable gift.

Mehdigulu Khan

Ibrahim Khan, as we are going to describe later in the book, was killed by the Russians during the Russo-Azerbaijani wars. His son Mehdigulu Khan fought long and bloody wars against the Russian aggressors. However, the whole Khanate was annexed by Russia in 1806.

Other Khanates

There were other Khanates in Mughan besides Karabakh: Ganja, Irevan, Nakhichevan and Lenkoran. The power of these states extended

---

[45] The real assassins of Qajar Shah are not known for certain. It is believed that his own serviceman by the name of Sadiq Khan murdered Qajar in his tent in Shusha.

over the territories that were approximately the same size as the areas of the present-day provinces of Ganja, Irevan[46], Nakhichevan and Lenkoran.

The Final Years of the Khanates

The Situation before and during the Russian Invasion

Shirvan (Shemakha) Khanate

The new Iranian king Nadir Shah massacred most of the residents of Shemakha and exiled the rest of them to the city of Aghsu. After the retreat of Nadir Shah, a khan by the name of Mohammed Ali bey became the ruler in "New Shemakha", and two other khans Mohammed Said bey and Aghasi bey seized the power in "Old Shemakha". Under the Iranian shah Kerimkhan Zend who replaced Nadir shah at the throne Mohammed Said bey invaded "New Shemakha" and defeated Mohammed Eli bey.

While the khans in Shirvan were feuding with each other the khan of Quba Fetheli Khan stabilized the situation in Shemakha and returned the exiled residents to the city. Fetheli Khan arranged the marriage of his daughter and Mohammed Said bey whom he made the sovereign in Shemakha. However, Mohammed's brother Aghasi resumed an armed struggle again. In the end, Fetheli Khan had both brothers hanged thus merging Shemakha with his Khanate. The supporters of the brothers escaped to Karabakh. In 1793, they entered Shemakha and toppled the local ruler. Although two people from the nobility, Asghar Khan and Gasim Khan, were vying for the throne Aghasi bey's son Mustafa Khan was victorious in claiming the crown.

The Iranian Shah Agha Mohammed Shah Qajar looted Shemakha in 1794. Mustafa had to retreat to the Fit (Caucasian) mountain. Later he descended from the mountains to his native city. Mustafa Khan was a very simple man. He despised jewelry, expensive clothes, and other attributes of the rich. Mustafa Khan would wear plain clothes looking almost like a dervish. Although he preferred to live in a tent his viziers lived in splendid

---

[46] After the Russian occupation of the Irevan Khanate a massive migration of Armenians from the Ottoman Empire and Iran changed the demographics of the province so that in the second half of the 19th century almost half of the population were Armenians whereas they had been a tiny minority before the Russian conquest. Irevan was renamed Yerevan in the early 20th century and became the capital of Armenia. Throughout the 20th century, ethnic cleansing of Azerbaijanis from the Irevan Khanate now known as the Armenian Republic resulted in all Azerbaijanis being expelled from their native lands (The publisher's note).

palaces and buildings. The people always highly valued Mustafa's such attitude.

Mustafa Khan established good relations with the government in Derbend and annexed Salyan. However, his relations with the Khan of Karabakh and the Iranian Shah were very tense. He even threatened a messenger of the Shah once. Then Mustafa attacked Qajar Shah's army that was returning from the Georgian campaign and captured 3 or 4 Russian-made cannons. He sent these weapons to Russia as a gesture of goodwill. In return, the "grateful" Russians under the command of General Zubov launched an offensive against Shemakha and occupied the city in 1795. Mustafa had to move into the Fit mountains again. The Russians installed Gasim bey in Shemakha. Only in 1798 that is after Russia's withdrawal did Mustafa Khan restore his authority in the city.

The Khanate of Sheki

In 1713, Haji Chelebi was in charge of Sheki Khanate. His son Hussein Khan replaced him after his death in 1772.

Nukha (the old name of Sheki) was a naturally fortified city in the shape of a fortress. Very few aggressors who invaded the Azerbaijani lands could capture this castle. Even Nadir Shah who occupied all of Azerbaijan failed to take Sheki. Only Agha Mohammed Shah Qajar did succeed in his war effort against Sheki. Despite the strong resistance on the part of the Sheki Khan Mohammed Hasan Khan the Iranians stormed and seized the city. Mohammed Hasan Khan's eyes were put out for his attempt to fight the Shah. Mohammed Hasan Khan returned to Nukha after Qajar's withdrawal to Iran.

This Sheki Khan married one of the Georgian princesses. Under the pressure of his Georgian father-in-law, the Russian influence which was already present in Tiflis began spreading into Sheki Khanate.

The Khanate of Ganja

Shahverdi Khan, a member of the Qajar family (Iranian Shah Qajar was ethnic Azerbaijani), was in power in Ganja at that time. Ganja was under constant attacks from Karabakh. Shahverdi Khan requested the help of the Georgian King who assisted Shahverdi to stop the Karabakh onslaughts. However, Shahverdi Khan was murdered during a rebellion in Ganja, and his supporters had to escape to Georgia. Irakli, the Georgian King, crushed the revolt and installed Shahverdi's youngest son. That year the Kurds and Lezghins incited another mutiny which was put down with the help of Irakli again. In 1795, the Russians entered Ganja for the first time, but they were easily repelled.

The Khanate of Baku

In 1724, the Russians under the command of general Matushkin occupied Baku and the surrounding areas. They made a certain Mahmud Dargha the mayor of the city. The Russian troops stripped the local population of the weapons and then settled in two major Caravanserais in Baku. The mosques were converted into prisons. Naturally, under these conditions, no one was going to tolerate the Russian presence. Even Mahmud Dargha began secret talks with the Ottomans who were in Shemakha at that time. The Russians found out about the secret dealings of Mahmud Dargha, and Mahmud had to stay in Shemakha to avoid punishment. However, the Russians were too angry at the residents of Baku for their civil disobedience. The Russian commanders decided to carry out a massacre of the civilian population in Baku. The ones who avoided death were exiled to central Russia. The only civilians left in the city were Armenian and Indian merchants who happened to be in Baku on business trips. Russia moved a large number of Tartars from different parts of Russia to Baku.

In 1733, the Russians had to pull out of Baku. The survivors of the exile were now able to return to Baku. No sooner had the unfortunate Baku residents begun rebuilding after this genocide from the Russians than the Iranians struck the city. Nadir Shah undertook a military campaign against Baku and appointed his officer Gelem Khan from Gilan the mayor of Baku. After Nadir Shah's withdrawal Gelem Khan was overthrown, and a local warrior by the name of Mohammed Khan was brought to power. In 1759, he died and was replaced by his son Malik Mohammed Khan. In 1795, the Russian general Zubov attacked Baku with large forces, but as a result of the heroic defense of Baku residents, the Russian army was defeated and forced to retreat.

The Khanate of Quba

In that period Quba was ruled by the Qaragalpag khans. In 1726, the Russians occupied the Khanate and made an eight-year old Ali bey the ruler. Ali bey was removed immediately after the Russian retreat.

In 1759, Fetheli Khan became the sovereign in Quba. It was at this time that the people of Derbend were languishing under the oppressive rule of Mohammed Hussein Khan. The population would support anyone who would rid them of the hated khan. Fetheli Khan decided to take advantage of such favorable conditions and besiege Derbend. The siege lasted two months and ended with the arrest of Mohammed Khan together with his son. Thus, Fetheli Khan now ruled Derbend in addition to Salyan that he had conquered earlier. Fetheli Khan arranged the wedding of his daughter and the Khan of Baku, therefore gaining influence in Baku. Later, as we have already mentioned he occupied Shemakha. Fetheli Khan became so powerful that at some point he was contemplating a campaign against Iran.

He died in 1771. His son Shikheli Khan became the Khan of Quba. Such was the situation in the Khanates of Azerbaijan. We shall describe the political situation in Khanates such as Lenkoran, Irevan, Nakhichevan and other small Azerbaijani Khanates later in the book.

Azerbaijan during the Khanate Era
Art, Education and Literature

Azerbaijan has suffered numerous aggressions throughout its history because of its strategic geographic location. Although most of their time the Azerbaijanis were busy fighting invaders, they still found time and opportunity to create masterpieces in science, literature and other fields of arts. Besides these achievements, Azerbaijan gave birth to a number of world-renowned literary giants. Here is one of them who became famous during the Khanate period.

Vagif

A great and fiery poet by the name of Molla Penah became extremely popular in Karabakh under the penname of Vagif. He was originally from the city of Qazakh (northwestern Azerbaijan) but spent all of his life in Karabakh.

He had struggled most of his life until 1761 when Ibrahim Khan, the ruler of Karabakh, took Vagif into his palace. Thus, Vagif's monetary problems were solved. He became so popular all over Azerbaijan that the saying "Everyone who goes to school can't be Molla Penah ..." is still used by Azerbaijanis today.

Molla Penah Vagif's Mausoleum in Shusha, Azerbaijan (Now severely damaged by the Armenian armed forces after the occupation of Karabakh region of Azerbaijan in 1991-92)

Vagif wrote primarily in styles of mukhemmes and murebbe which were rare in Azerbaijan at the time. In 1796 when Agha Mohammed Shah Qajar invaded Karabakh, Ibrahim Khan had to retreat to Jarbelakan. The Iranians arrested Vagif together with his son. The Iranians were ruthless killing people indiscriminately. Even the Ottoman messenger who arrived in Shusha to inform the Shah of the Turkish intent to protect Karabakh was executed at once. Vagif and his son were supposed to share the same fate the following day. Luckily, Qajar was murdered, and the great poet's life was saved.

Later in that period Vagif and his son were executed by Mohammed bey Gilij Batman who was fighting for power in Karabakh. Vagif was buried in a place known as "Dilgusha" in Shusha. Even today the young women and girls visit his grave every year on a day called "last Wednesday" to commemorate the great poet.

Trade and Industry. Azerbaijan has always been the commercial center of the region. Its geographic situation and active trade with India strengthened its position as a well-developed country. Today's East-West trade is still carried out through the same routes.

Ganja was the most important trade center. Shemakha was also active in commerce although its main partner at that time was Russia. In 1711, when the Lezghins attacked Shemakha they claimed to see almost three hundred Russian merchants whose total merchandise was valued to be four million manats. This enormous amount of wealth was a strong indicator of the huge volume of trade between Azerbaijan and Russia.

The oil resources of Azerbaijan were not fully utilized yet. Oil was extracted manually using large pails. Then it was poured into barrels for export. Before the Russian occupation of Ganja, there were approximately four hundred factories manufacturing glass, silk and metals in the city including its suburbs Bayan, Siyeh and Daghkesen.

Taxes. During the Khans' rule in Azerbaijan, most businesses were taxed. However, we do not have precise data on how much was levied on a particular trade. It is known with certainty, however, that when the Russians captured Ganja the annual tax revenues of the Khanate were fifty thousand manats. Below are taxes imposed on various industries.

Industries	Taxes
Leather painters	3700 manats
Weights and Measurement tax	1500
Slaughter Houses	1600
Butchers	900
Bathhouses	300
Customs Office	3000
Bread makers	120
Glass merchants	160
Eating Places	300
Clothing Merchants	220
Leather Traders	200
Fruit Merchants	3000
Soap Sellers	800
Wine Makers	230
Tobacco Manufacturers	120
and so on.	

The fact that only 120 manats were collected from the bread makers shows a reasonable level of taxation in the Khanate.

Measurements

There were no standard measurements used in all the Azerbaijani Khanates. Every city, even every village had its own measurement system. Although it was partially borrowed from Anatolia, and partially taken from Iran, the bulk of measurements was primarily invented and adopted by the local authorities and merchants.

The only common measurement accepted throughout Azerbaijan was "yuk" (means a load or weight in Azerbaijani) which was equivalent to 164 kilos. The "aghaj" (means a tree in Azerbaijani) was used to measure the distance. One Aghaj was approximately 7 kilometers.

In commerce, a smaller unit was used known as "kez" or "arshin". Arshin was equal to the following in the metric system in different cities: Baku (99 cm), Ganja (105 cm), Quba (72 cm), Nakhichevan (103 cm). These measurements are still used in provinces and villages, while the residents of Baku also use "behre" and "kirch". The Russian measurement systems are used nowadays in cities but are not so popular in the countryside.

Coins

Not all the coins minted in the Azerbaijani Khanates are known, however, most of them are still available today. During the Russian invasion of Ganja, there were following coins with the following exchange rates: One silver manat (85 Russian kopeks), One silver abbasi (17 Russian kopeks), One gold coin worth ten shahilig (42 Russian kopeks), One bagir shah (0.5 Russian kopeks).

In addition to these, the coins of other Khanates such as Karabakh, Sheki, Shirvan and others were in circulation in Ganja. Here are some examples of the coins minted in the abovementioned Khanates and their Russian currency equivalent: In Karabakh: One silver penavat (20 Russian kopeks), Sheki: One silver tenke (20 Russian kopeks), Shirvan: one silver penavat (15 Russian kopeks).

Iranian grans and Russian silver rubles were also in circulation in Azerbaijan.

Historical Monuments under the Azerbaijani Khans

Shemakha

Most important industrial and cultural buildings in Shemakha were destroyed as a result of periodic earthquakes. Such large mosques as "Div Ali", "Jamei-Kabir" and others were burned down with the rest of the city by the Armenian Dashnak armed gangs in 1918.

Sheki

The ancient Nukha was surrounded by huge fortress walls. A beautiful palace and a small elegant mosque that were inside the fortress survived to our day. The palace was built by the Sheki Khan Mohammed Hasan Khan in 1694. The Russians converted the mosque into a church after their occupation of the city. After Azerbaijan declared its independence in 1918, the building became a mosque again.

Sheki Khan's Palace, Sheki, Azerbaijan

Ganja

A splendid mosque constructed by Shah Abbas in 1605 boasts two wonderful and tall minarets in the center of Ganja. The mosque was partially damaged during the war of Karabakh but was restored by Javad Khan in 1793.

Ganja Khan Palace, Azerbaijan

The shrine of Ibrahim from the Tahire Dynasty which is located seven kilometers to the north of Ganja is still a major attraction. There is also a shrine of the great Azerbaijani poet Sheikh Nizami Ganjavi (12th century) three kilometers from Ganja towards Karabakh. Unfortunately, there are no ruins of many great palaces, castles, mosques and other buildings that were routinely constructed in Ganja.

Baku

The present-day city of Baku is divided into two parts: New City and Old City. Old Baku is surrounded by a stone fortress with many gates. Old Baku is known among the local residents as "Qala" (means "Stronghold" in Azerbaijani) or "Icheri Sheher" (literally "Inner City"). There is the "Palace of the Khan" that was the residence of Baku Khans in the Inner City. A marvelous mosque called the "Mosque of Shah" that was built by the Khan of Shirvan Khalilullah Khan the First in 1449 is also located in this medieval complex. Baku also boasts a famous "Maiden Tower", a unique castle that was mentioned earlier in the book. One can also see the ruins of an ancient Zoroastrian temple called Ateshgah (see Part One) in the village of Surakhani to the west of Baku. It is the only fire worshiping temple left from a huge number of these pre-Islamic shrines on the territory of Azerbaijan. The eternal fires are still on in this Ateshgah. If we take into consideration that our country is called Azerbaijan, that is, according to some sources, the land of fire, we come to appreciate how important the study of this last shrine is.

Karabakh

Today there are many ruins known as "City places" scattered across Mughan and Karabakh. The archeological findings such as ancient pillars, pipes, stones, and other objects indicate that these desolate sites used to be large and lively cities. Russian archeologists have found dozens of treasures, windmill stones, etc. in the same areas. The hills where these items are found were named "The Hill of Money", " The Village of Windmill". Besides these sites, there are also hills known as "Gold", "Marriage", "Yellow Sand", "Windmill Nose" and so on which need to be researched. These archeological sites undoubtedly hold the key to a great deal of data on our glorious and heroic past. Only the Fortress of Askeran did survive to our day from the period of Khanates. This stronghold is situated on the route from Aghdam to Shusha serving as a gate to Karabakh. A significant effort was exerted to construct the irrigation system in Mughan. However, only mere traces of the canals are found today. In Mughan some of the waterways have been repaired and are currently used by farms. A large number of these water canals is a strong indication of the enormous wealth of ancient Azerbaijan.

There is a tower called "Gunbez" in the west of Barda. Although it contains many inscriptions on its walls, they are practically illegible. Professor Khanikov managed to read only the date of "1321" on Gunbez. Unfortunately, Gunbez is doomed to destruction just like the Shemkir Fortress which has been reduced to the ground. In 1825, the German scientist Ekvald studied the Shemkir Fortress. However, in 1859, the French professor Dori could not even detect the traces of that stronghold. It is regrettable that the historical heritage of our ancestors is disappearing because of our negligence.

The Govheraga Mosque, built in the 18th Century, in Shusha, Azerbaijan, now severely damaged after the Armenian occupation of Karabakh

Nakhichevan

The ancient city of Nakhichevan used to be to the west of the modern city. Only the ruins of that magnificent city do remain today. There is also a tower in the city dating back to the Khanate era. It is believed to have been designed as a possible shrine for the Khan of Nakhichevan.

Nakhichevan Khan Palace, Nakhichevan, Azerbaijan

Irevan

The city was surrounded by defense walls. The stone walls erected by the Ottomans in 1552 are still intact. Irevan also boasts splendid palaces and mosques besides the fortress walls. The most important ones are a large mosque constructed by Penah Khan, the khan of Irevan in 1686, and the "Blue Mosque" built by Husseyn Ali Khan in 1764. The visitors also enjoy the view of the ruins of the Fortress Mosque that is located inside the Irevan Stronghold[47].

Wall decorations in Irevan's Sardar Palace (destroyed after Armenia took over Irevan)

---

[47] Regrettably, after a mass migration of Armenians to Irevan this city eventually became the capital city of the Armenian Republic in 1918. In the decades following that event, the city's historic center has been gradually demolished by the Armenian authorities and almost all Azerbaijani architectural heritage except for the Blue Mosque has been destroyed. The Azerbaijanis who founded and populated Irevan since its establishment were expelled from Irevan by the successive Armenian governments during several ethnic cleansing campaigns in the 20th century (The publisher's note).

PART SIX

The Russian Yoke (1827-1916)
The Occupation of Azerbaijan by Russia

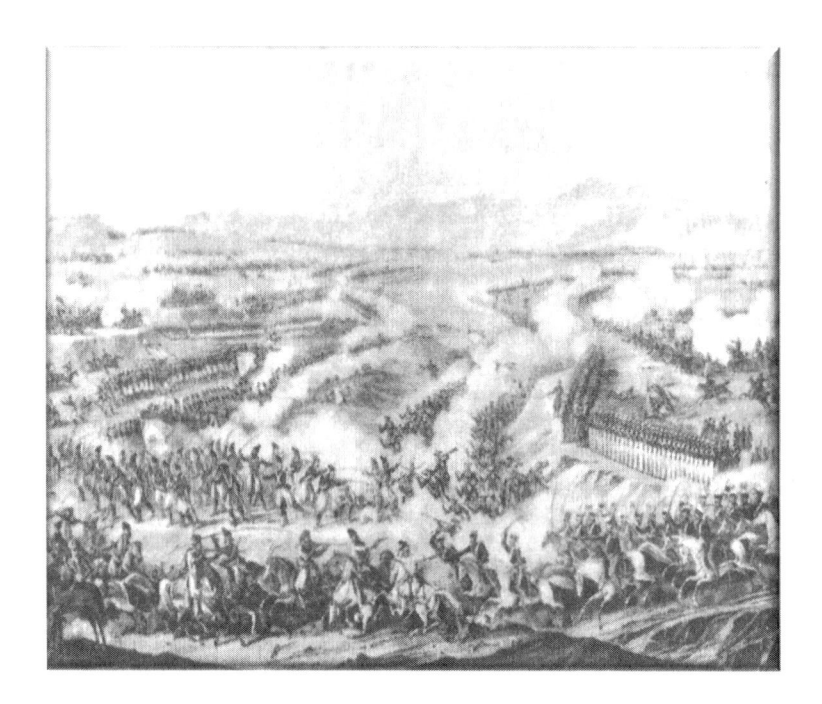

The Russians had been trying to invade Azerbaijan through Derbend and occupy our country since ancient times. These attempts were made as far back in history as during the Arab domination in Azerbaijan. The Russian historian Nestor writes about Russian military campaigns in Azerbaijan in 965. The famous Russian adventurer Stenka Razin also invaded Azerbaijan. It should also be noted that the Moscow kingdom tended to use arranged marriages with the Caucasian nobility in order to expand its influence in that region. For instance, Izyaslav the Second married the daughter of the Abkhazian Khan; Czar George married the Georgian Princess Tamara, and Ivan the Terrible, yet another Russian king, married a Circassian woman.

The Russians had been coming to Caucasus and Azerbaijan for both aggressive and peaceful purposes. This movement towards the Caucasus accelerated the demise of ill-fated Khanates of Kazan (the capital of Tatarstan) and Ezhderkhan (*today known as Astrakhan which used to be the center of the Astrakhan Khanate occupied by Russia in 1556*). Exactly 300 years after the Russian conquest of these Khanates Azerbaijan found itself in the Russian yoke too.

The wars that the Russians waged against Iran and the Ottomans also contributed to the occupation of Azerbaijan. Azerbaijan was the first target in the Russian plans to conquer the Caucasus and Anatolia and secure a foothold on the Bosporus Strait thus getting access to the Mediterranean. As a result of these conflicts, Iran and the Ottomans were weakened and pushed away from Azerbaijan. And despite sixty years of the heroic resistance by the Caucasian peoples against Russia the region was eventually subdued. Besides these factors, Christian Georgia also assisted Russia in its expansionist policies by inviting them to the Caucasus. The Georgians had been longing for the Russian protection for years. Finally, in 1800, Russia took Georgia under its wing and sent the troops to Tiflis. At this time Sheikh Shamil was fighting bloody battles with the Russian aggressors in the north of the Caucasus, while the Azerbaijani Khans were locked in deadly conflicts with the Russian imperialists in the south.

After the Russian troops had been stationed in Georgia Sheikh Shamil's communications with the Ottomans were completely cut off, and a sixty-year heroic stance of the North Caucasians ended with the occupation of Daghestan in 1858 and Circassia in 1863. The Russians also subjugated the Azerbaijani Khanates.

The campaigns of Peter the First. This Russian Czar invaded Azerbaijan via the Caspian Sea and captured Derbend, Tarki and Anji Qala. However, a terrible storm that began in the Caspian sank thirty Russian warships in the Sea and thirteen warships that were docked in the Derbend harbor. Peter left a large army detachment in Derbend and went to Astrakhan. This Russian expeditionary corps took over Baku. However, a peace treaty with Iran dictated the withdrawal of this Russian force from Azerbaijan. The reason for this decision was large-scale rebellions in Azerbaijan and Daghestan and the Iran-Ottoman wars.

The Campaigns of Katherine. In 1795, the Russian Queen Katherine the Second sent a large force into Azerbaijan under the pretext of a war with the Ottomans and defense of Georgia from Iran. Generals Agverdiyev and Zubov were commanders of this army. The Russians occupied Daghestan and approached Azerbaijani city Derbend. The khan of Derbend Sheikh Ali Khan and his brave sister Perije Khatun heroically defended the city. However, after a long siege, the city fell. After the conquest of such a strong city as Derbend the Khanates of Baku, Quba and Shemakha surrendered to Zubov's army. Only Karabakh and Sheki Khanates did not lay down their weapons and tried to assassinate Zubov via Sheikh Ali Khan. Zubov managed to occupy all of Azerbaijan and even Gilan province in Iran. Then the Russian forces set out to capture Tehran. But Katherine died in 1796 bringing the war to an abrupt end. The new Russian Czar Paul was not a war hawk and immediately ordered the army back to Russia. Zubov began pulling his troops back to the Terek River. The Russian army suffered great losses at the hands of the local population during their withdrawal from Azerbaijan.

The Dark Days of Azerbaijan

After the Russian occupation of the independent Georgian principalities of Kartli and Kakhetia in 1800, the freedom of Azerbaijan was jeopardized too. At the same time, the Russians occupied Akhsekhe and Jarbelakan. Although the Russians entered Georgia under the pretext of protection, they had no intention of stopping there. The Russian commander Tsitsianov led his troops against Ganja.

The War of Ganja

Ganja was the main gate into Azerbaijan from the west. The Russians claimed that their move against Ganja was to force Ganja to pay the outstanding tributes to Georgia. But the real reason for this invasion was to cut Ganja and Azerbaijan off from Iran.

In 1802, Tsitsianov personally led his troops to Ganja and demanded that Javad Khan, the khan of Ganja, capitulate at once. The hero of Ganja, however, responded with the following words: " ...Your end must have come. You will soon witness that..." The Russians began a long siege of the city. During the siege, the Russians sent numerous letters to Javad Khan urging him to surrender the city. Javad Khan repeatedly rejected this demand. He wrote in one of his reply letters:" Who in the world has seen that a Russian could be more courageous than a Turk?". Finally, he answered angrily to the Russian ultimatums with " ...as long as I live on this earth Ganja will never surrender".

The siege was getting more intense. The Russians also launched a fierce offensive on the Karabakh gates of the city using the cannon fire. They were brutally beaten back. Javad Khan would arrive at the point of the offensive and personally command the defending force. The second large Russian attack was repulsed with great casualties on both sides. The Russians undertook the third attack. This time some treacherous Armenians from Ganja conspired with the Russian generals. The Tiflis gates of the city came under a surprise attack. Javad Khan immediately took over the defense in that section of the fortress. Unfortunately, this great warrior fell in this battle together with his son. After the death of this heroic son of Azerbaijan, the spirit of the defenders was broken, and the Russians entered the city on January 4, 1804. The Russians were met with fierce street fighting which finally resulted in the Russian occupation of the city.

The Tomb of Javad Khan, Ganja, Azerbaijan Republic

The Consequences of the Ganja War

The heroic and fierce defense of Ganja angered the Russians most. That is why they changed the name of the city to Yelizavetpol in honor of the Russian Queen after they had seized it. After the collapse of such a strong Azerbaijani Khanate as Ganja other smaller Khanates were doomed to surrender. Small west Georgian principalities such as Mingrel, Imeret and Guriya capitulated to Russia without any resistance. The conquest of Ganja facilitated further Russian occupation of the Azerbaijani Khanates.

It is noteworthy that the Khan of Sheki Selim Khan surrendered to the Russians only because of his fear of the Khan of Shirvan. Instead of uniting their forces to fight the Russian invasion, the khans were embroiled in internal feuds thus weakening their own capabilities to organize an effective defense. Although practically all of the Khans understood that mistake it was too late to put up an effective fight against the Russian army.

Political and Military Developments (1802-1805)

After the fall of Ganja, the Russians moved to the south and captured Qara Kilse and Ejmiadzin. At the request of Mohammed Khan, the ruler of Irevan, the Iranian Prince Abbas Mirze sent his close general Mohammed Shefi Khan from Tabriz to help the Irevan Khanate. Abbas Mirze also instructed Mehdigulu Khan to make sure that the Kengerli and Qajar tribes move from Kars to Azerbaijan in order to boost the support for Irevan. These tribes settled around Irevan.

The First War of Irevan. On the news of possible Iranian assistance to the Irevan Khanate, the Russians sped up their move towards the city. Abbas Mirze also arrived with his army from Iran and set up his camp near "Qirkhbulaq" ("Forty Springs"). The Qazakh and Shemseddinli tribes joined the Iranian forces. After a minor clash with the Russians, the position of the Iranian-Azerbaijani army was weakened, and it was forced to retreat to Sadarak, in Nakhichevan.

The Russians surrounded Irevan and began bombarding the city using heavy artillery. But despite this brutal attack on Irevan the Azerbaijanis bravely rolled the Russians back. Abbas Mirze immediately reported the serious situation in Irevan to the Iranian Shah who dispatched a force under the command of Ismail bey Damghanli (also an Azerbaijani) from the city of Sultaniyye. A savage battle with the Russians ensued. Aligulu Khan from the Shahseven tribe, Pirgulu Khan from the Qajars and the local residents of Irevan defeated the aggressors. Irevan could breathe freely after two months of the Russian siege. The Russian casualties were four thousand people. They were forced to retreat to Tiflis. The retreating Russian troops left a big haul. Abbas Mirze let Mohammed Khan and Kelbeli Khan rule Irevan and Nakhichevan respectively and returned to Iran.

The Campaign of Karabakh. Abbas Mirze launched attacks against Ibrahim khan of Karabakh because he cooperated with the Russians. Abbas Mirze ordered Ismail bey to march his troops against Ibrahim in 1804.

Ibrahim Khan in his turn sent his son Mohammed Hasan Khan to counter the advancing troops of Ismail bey. They clashed twenty kilometers to the north of the Khudaferin bridge. After having been informed of the approaching troops of Abbas Mirze, Mohammed Khan decided his numbers were insufficient to fight such a large force and pulled his army back to Shusha. Abbas Mirze meanwhile was moving through Aghoghlan-Chinaqchi and ran into the Russian troops near Askeran. Abbas Mirze cornered the Russians who were commanded by Kariagin and Kotlyarovski. The Russians kept switching their positions between Kebristan and Ternaut, and finally, asked for four days to surrender. Abbas Mirze gave them permission. However, the Russians seized that respite to escape to Chehrigh Dagh where the Armenians resided. Abbas Mirze pursued the Russians and defeated another Russian division that arrived to reinforce the almost destroyed detachment. Finally, Abbas Mirze settled the conflict with Ibrahim Khan peacefully and rushed to Ganja.

The Events in Ganja. Abbas Mirze besieged Ganja after having ousted the Russians from Karabakh. The residents of the city spared no effort to help Abbas Mirze. However, the saboteurs spread false rumors about the intentions of the Iranian-Azerbaijani army. As a result of this provocation over six thousand people moved out of the city and settled near the camps of the army. This move affected the troops that were carrying out the siege, and they also returned to the camp. Therefore, Abbas Mirze changed his plans and pulled his army to Zeyem. Abbas Mirze arranged the transportation of the refugees from Ganja to Iran. He himself seized a Russian provision convoy traveling from Tiflis to Ganja and returned to Irevan.

The Death of Ibrahim Khan. Abbas Mirze was in Ardabil when Ibrahim, the khan of Karabakh, sent an envoy to Iran asking Abbas Mirze to completely drive the Russians out of Azerbaijan. Abbas Mirze sent Ferejullah Khan and Abulfet Khan with the Shahseven tribes and followed them with his own army. But when he reached the Khudaferin bridge Abbas received the news of the tragic murder of Ibrahim khan and his whole family. A Russian military unit executed Ibrahim Khan and his family near Shusha. He was killed because of his links with the Iranians. This news seriously distressed the entire population of Karabakh, and the Karabakh tribes decided not to live under the Russian oppression and prepared to leave for Iran. Abbas Mirze instructed Ataullah Khan from the Shahsevens to organize the immigration of the Karabakh residents to Iran. Then Abbas Mirze together with the Afshar, Qajar, Shahseven and other Turkic tribes entered Mughan. As soon as Abbas arrived in Mughan he was informed of a large concentration of the Russian troops in Askeran which also included the Armenians who lived in Karabakh at the time. Abbas Mirze immediately struck the Russians. The battle occurred in Khankendi[48] and lasted two days, but neither side could gain the upper hand. The Iranian army had to withdraw to Iran because their supply lines were stretched thin.

The Battle of Jebrayil. When the Karabakh tribes began their migration to Iran the residents of Jebrayil did not even respond to their plight. Instead, they joined the Russians in the offensive on the protection force that was to provide the safety of the migrating people. The attack took place near Kapan. Abbas Mirze in his turn marched through Aslanduz and defeated the Russians forcing them to retreat to Ganja.

The Occupation of Baku

Taking advantage of the political fragmentation in Azerbaijan the Russians were conquering the Khanates one after another. Now it was the turn of unfortunate Baku. The Russian army led by general Zavalishin moved against the Baku Khanate in 1805. However, Zavalishin decided not to advance as soon as he was informed of the troops from Quba coming to help Baku. The unity of these two Azerbaijani Khanates forced a large Russian army to retreat. If only had all the Khanates of the motherland united like them Azerbaijan could undoubtedly have been liberated from the Russian occupation.

Regrettably, the feudal differences prevailed over the national interests and unity. General Tsitsianov, the Commander-in-Chief of the Russian occupational forces stationed in Tiflis, was extremely frustrated at the return of the troops under Zavalishin. He decided to lead the troops against Baku personally. In his letter to Husseyngulu Khan, the sovereign of Baku, he wrote that "I will either die or take Baku". The former came true. This Russian general failed to capture Baku Fortress and was killed near Baku.

---

[48] After the establishment of the Soviet power in Azerbaijan in 1920 Khankendi was renamed Stepanakert after Stepan Shaumyan, an Armenian Bolshevik, who spearheaded mass killings of the Azerbaijani civilians in Baku in 1918. The city is currently under the Armenian military occupation (The publisher's note).

Transcaucasia in the early XIX century

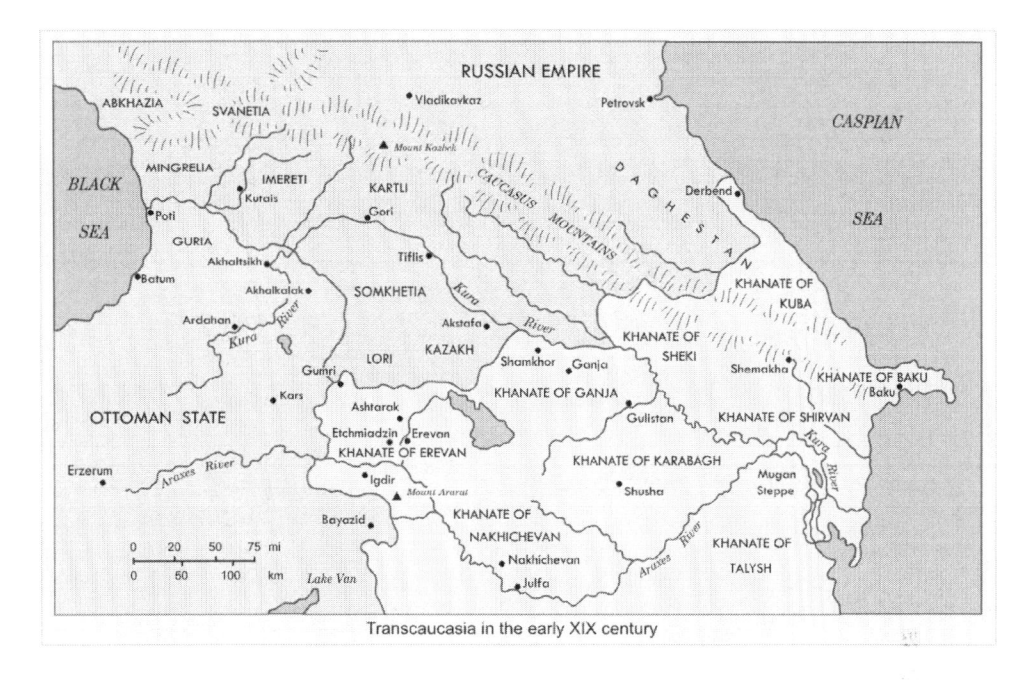

Meanwhile, Abbas Mirze sent one thousand Afshars to assist Baku's defenders. His general Ahmed Khan followed the Afshars to Baku. Abbas Mirze marched to Mughan. However, he received the following message from Pirgulu Khan, the commander of the infantry sent to fight in Shirvan: "The Russians signed an agreement with Shirvan and used their territory to launch an offensive on Baku. A Russian flotilla was constantly bombarding the city. However, as a result of the heroic resistance and counterattacks by the Azerbaijanis Tsitsianov was forced to offer peace. A storm in the Caspian also destroyed supplies bound for the Russian forces. Tsitsianov was plotting to invite the Khan of Baku to negotiations when he was assassinated during the meeting. The Russian army descended into chaos and retreated." Abbas Mirze considered further movement unnecessary and went back to Iran. But a year later the Russians were back at Baku suburbs again. This time they occupied the city on July 3, 1806. The body of Tsitsianov who was buried in Baku was transferred to Tiflis. After the investigation into his assassination, it was determined that the Khan of Baku had nothing to do with it. The murder was organized by Emin Hemze, the son of the late Khan of Karabakh, to revenge his father's and family's murder at the hands of the Russian troops.

The Consequences of the Occupation of Baku

After Baku, the enemy easily conquered Quba.
The Russians strengthened their position in Daghestan.
The Russians secured their supremacy in the Caspian
Sea.

The Political and Military Situation (1806-1812)
The Clashes in Sheki and Shirvan

The peace agreement between the Russians and the Khan of Shirvan was the cause of the Iranian fury. Abbas Mirze ordered Hussein Qajarli Khan to lead his troops into Shirvan. Abbas Mirze chose a route via Aslanduz to enter Mughan. The Khan of Shirvan appointed his brother Ismail bey to guard the banks of the Kura River. However, after a small skirmish with the Iranians, the latter forded the river and occupied Shirvan. Mustafa Khan, the ruler of Shirvan, retreated to the Fit Mountain. The Iranian attempts to catch him failed. Mustafa Khan was repeatedly invited to come to Shemakha for negotiations, but he refused. Abbas Mirze sent Mohammed Ali bey to initiate talks with the Khan. Abbas himself marched to Shirvan via Aghsu and after a short siege seized the city. He moved all of the residents to Mughan.

Finally, Selim Khan, the lord of Sheki, brokered peace between Iran and Shirvan. However, the peace did not last long as the rumors were spread regarding an Iranian plot to arm Selim's brother and pit him against Selim Khan. In response, Selim Khan began guerrilla warfare from the Kulsis Mountain. The rumors were started by the Shirvan ruler, so the Iranians sent a messenger to assure Selim Khan of the Iranian support.

Abbas Mirze meanwhile was planning a campaign against Derbend, but the Russian treaty with the Khan of Derbend prevented him from carrying out his plan. Then a terrible case of jaundice erupted in Aghsu and claimed a huge number of Iranian troops. Abbas Mirze returned to Tabriz. On his way to Tabriz Mustafa khan of Shirvan attacked Abbas' troops and destroyed the Iranian forces that were in the rearguard.

The Shirvan Migration. After the Russians occupied Shirvan many people there did not want to suffer under the Russian rule and moved to Mughan and Talish under the protection of Pirgulu Khan Qajarli (an ethnic Azerbaijani as well). Mustafa Khan tried to turn the migrating people back but failed. He marched together with the Russians all the way to Salyan in an effort to bring the people back, but the Iranian army rolled them back.

The Occupation of Sheki. Selim Khan of Sheki knew that the Russian plans included the occupation of Sheki after the fall of Baku, Shirvan and Derbend. That is why Selim Khan requested and received funds from Iran and reinforced his troops with the warriors from the Avar, Jar, Tle, Lezghin tribes of Daghestan. He fought two large wars with the Russians defeating them in both. However, the discipline among the Daghestanis was weak and soon they were gone. Selim Khan preferred to retreat to Iran to resisting a new Russian onslaught. The Russians entered Nukha and annexed the Khanate to Russia in 1807.

The Siege of Irevan. When the Russians attacked Irevan the Khan of Irevan Hussein Khan Qajarli met them with his army and some armed Kurds. However, the Kurds were disorganized, and soon Hussein Khan returned to Irevan. The Russians laid siege to the city. Abbas Mirze in his turn sent Ferejullah khan and Emenullah khan with troops from the Afshars to help Irevan. However, they could not break through the Russian lines and had to return to Iran. At the same time, another Russian army marched through Karabakh and Qarababa to Nakhichevan and occupied the city. Abbas Mirze moved via Khoy and reached Nakhichevan inflicting big losses on the Russian forces. However, the majority of the Nakhichevanis migrated to the village of Deresham to the south of the Arax. That is why Abbas retreated to Qapanbasan. The Russians entered Nakhichevan again.

The stronghold of Irevan was well fortified and sustaining the ongoing Russian assaults. The defense of the city was also reinforced by the brother of the Irevan khan, Hasan khan, and such Turkic emirs as Kelbeli khan, Alinaghi khan and Ashraf khan. The Russians intensified the offensive by heavy bombardment of the city. Then they approached the city walls and erected the ladders to scale the walls. However, the attack was repulsed. The Russians lost thousands of men and set on fleeing. Hasan khan together with Ismail khan Qajarli began pursuing the remnants of the Russian army all the way to Georgia.

After this success of the Azerbaijanis Abbas Mirze gathered the cavalry and infantry from other Turkic tribes such as the Afshars, Khemse and Chardolu and marched towards Nakhichevan. The Russians left the city without any resistance and went to Qarababa. Kerim bey Kengerli was assigned to pursue the enemy, and Ahmed Khan was in charge of cutting off the fleeing Russian troops in the place called Salvarti. The foe began fleeing from the area as soon as they discovered the Azerbaijani plans. Thus, Irevan and Nakhichevan were delivered from Russian aggression, and Abbas Mirze returned to Tabriz.

The War of Zeyem (1808). Abbas Mirze dispatched Abulfat Khan of Javanshir andBeydilli khan from Karabakh on a reconnaissance mission to Baku. Abbas himself arrived in Goyche Lake area (today also known as Sevan lake) via Ordubad, Nakhichevan and Sherur. Abbas met baron Verdi, a Russian envoy who came to negotiate peace and sent him to Tabriz. Abbas also instructed Pirgulu khan Qajarli and Qaragozlu Mohammed Khan to organize the Azerbaijani resistance movement in Ganja. Abbas Mirze's forces moved towards Ganja and clashed with the Russian troops near Zeyem. There was no clear victor in that battle, and the Russians pulled their forces back to Georgia, and the Iranian-Azerbaijani army returned to Irevan.

The Conflict of Talish. Mustafa khan, the ruler of Talish and Lenkoran, signed a treaty with the Russians which angered Abbas Mirze. Ferejullah khan Afsharli was dispatched overland while Gilan forces attacked Lenkoran from the Caspian Sea. Although Mustafa khan fortified his positions near Jamish hoping for assistance from the Russians and Shirvan, the Iranians surrounded his position. Luckily, bloodshed was avoided due to the efforts of Mustafa khan's uncle Kune Seyin who brokered peace between the two sides. The khan of Lenkoran also sent his son to Shirvan to conclude peace with that Khanate.

Pillage and Emigration. As we have already mentioned earlier, during these wars Iran was constantly trying to move the Turkic tribes and peoples from Azerbaijan in order to deprive the Russians of the source of food and other supplies. Thus, in 1809, the tribes of Karabakh were transported to Qaradagh and the tribe of Irmeli was moved from Ganja to Nakhichevan. An Iranian official in charge of the migration of the Shemseddinli tribes of Qazakh plundered those tribes on their refusal to move to Iran.

At one point, Ibrahim khan Qajarli arrived in Mughan to set up a military force, but upon his failure he pillaged Karabakh and returned to Aslanduz. Later Qajarli Pirgulu khan and Qaragozlu Mohammed khan crossed the Terter River with the same purpose and looted the tribe of Jebrayil. The tribes of Chelebyanli and Yuzganli were moved to the south of the Arax.

In 1810, an armed group under Nezereli khan Kengerli moved most of the Karabakh population to Nakhichevan. Then Pirgulu khan Qajarli who was directing the migration of the Jebrayil tribe moved the tribes of Kolan and Mugaviz to Irevan and Nakhichevan.

In 1811 the Russians were wary of the intentions of the Jebrayil tribes to completely move to Iran just like the Emirli tribe had done before them. They began taking hostages from those tribes in order to stop the migration. Finally, most of these tribes did move to Iran. Jaffargulu khan, who moved to Iran together with his tribe on his own will, was appointed the ruler of Qaradagh with a salary of four thousand tumen.

The Iran-Ottoman Union. At this point, the Iranians and the Ottomans clearly understood the far-reaching consequences of the Russian expansionist designs, and they signed a peace treaty. Unfortunately, this union did not last long. An assassination attempt by a certain Kurd on the life of the Ottoman Commander of Kars Emin pasha marred the relations between the two countries. Abbas Mirze tried his best to show his sympathy to the Turkish commander by sending his personal doctor Monsieur Kemeli to treat Emin Pasha and special envoys to the Ottoman court. However, the rift between them remained.

The Treaty of Bekresh. In 1811, the Iranian-Azerbaijani army liberated Karabakh from the Russians and approached another Azerbaijani city, Ganja. The Russians acted urgently on the Ottoman front by signing a peace treaty with Istanbul according to which Anapa, Akhilkalak and Poti were to remain under Ottoman rule. The Russians needed this treaty in order to concentrate their forces against Iran. Nevertheless, the Russians suffered defeats at the wars near the Arax river and Aslanduz and had to retreat.

The War of Lenkoran

Lenkoran first accepted the Russian domination, but at later stages, they decided to side with the Iranians. That is why the Russians decided to revenge the Lenkoran residents and surrounded the city. Despite the Russian technological superiority, the brave people of Lenkoran fought against the Russian artillery and infantry with almost bare hands. The Russians finally took the city after a week-long siege on October 13th, 1811. But this occupation was a pyrrhic victory for Russia. Their forces suffered huge losses including two-thirds of the troops and the life of their commander Kotlyarovski.

In 1812, after the occupation of Lenkoran, the Russians halted military actions on the Azerbaijani front and signed a peace treaty known as the Gulustan Peace Treaty with Iran. Under the terms of this treaty, Iran accepted and recognized that Georgia, Daghestan, Karabakh, Ganja, Sheki, Shirvan, Derbend, Quba, Baku and Lenkoran Khanates became part of the Russian Empire.

Political Developments (1813-1822)

The Protection of Iran. Azerbaijan was turned into a bloodbath and lost hundreds of thousands of its sons and daughters in the wars against the Russian invaders. Despite all these sacrifices, Russia annexed ill-fated Azerbaijan. Nevertheless, the Azerbaijani people were not going to put up with that oppression and occupation of their motherland, and soon a large rebellion erupted in the country. At the same time as a result of the revolution in Iran Abbas Mirze became the Shah. He was a staunch Russophobe and provided all possible assistance to Azerbaijan. Abbas Mirze decided to appoint the former rulers of the Azerbaijani Khanates who immigrated to Iran the mayors of the border regions so that they could organize an effective resistance movement against the Russian occupants. Thus, Abbas appointed Husseynali khan of Balm and Georgian prince Alexander the mayors of the areas near the Russian annexed areas. Finally, in 1822, Iran had to declare war on Russia and set out on an offensive that resulted in taking Shureli Goz in Karabakh and besieging Shusha. But the Russians did not surrender, and the siege got protracted.

The Holy War of Azerbaijan. The entry of the Iranian army inspired the Azerbaijanis to begin a large-scale revolt against Russian rule. The people in the city of Luri in the Borchali region (today's eastern Georgia) rose against the Russians. In Ganja, armed residents attacked the Russian garrison at night and destroyed them thus freeing the city. The people of Baku invited Husseynali khan back to Baku. Surkhay khan in his turn entered Daghestan. The people all over Azerbaijan drove the Russians out and invited the former khans back. The Russians immediately pulled their troops from the Ottoman front and Georgia to Azerbaijan.

The War of Shemkir. On July 3 of the same year, a bloody battle occurred between the Iranians and the Russians near Shemkir. Emir khan, the Iranian commander, had to retreat leaving Ganja to the Russians. Abbas Mirze immediately abandoned the siege of Shusha and moved towards Ganja.

The War of Zazali. The Iranian army together with the Azerbaijani forces clashed with the Russian troops led by the general Paskevich who arrived to reinforce the Russian garrison in Ganja. The battle took place near an area called Zazali. On July 13, 1823, a horrific battle was fought in Zazali. The Russians outnumbered the allied forces, and Abbas Mirze was forced to retreat to Iran. The Russians managed to reoccupy some cities and villages. The Russian troops massacred the population of those places.

The War of Irevan and Nakhichevan

The proximity of these two Khanates to the Ottoman border and consequently their strategic importance doomed Irevan and Nakhichevan to the Russian occupation. On May 15, 1823, Mirze Abbas tried to break the siege of Irevan but failed. The Russian siege was not going according to plan as the Russians were short of cannons needed to bombard the walls of Irevan. On June 29th, the Russians attacked and seized Nakhichevan. After this, the invaders reinforced the siege of Irevan. The Russian army also defeated Abbas Mirze on the bank of the Javanbulag river. However, the Russian efforts to subdue Irevan did not yield results. The residents of Irevan were putting up a courageous fight.

Russian troops seizing the Irevan Fortress

The Russians tried to buy time in order to bring additional artillery and began peace talks with the Iranians. But the Iranian-Azerbaijani army routed the Russians under general Krasovski and freed Echmiadzin. Finally, the Russians delivered eighteen siege and twenty-two desert cannons to the Irevan area. They shelled and seized nearby Serdarabad fortress first. The Russians subjected Irevan to savage artillery bombardment that partially destroyed the defense walls and completely leveled many buildings in the city. The casualties among the civilians were catastrophic. In the end, after six days of incessant bombardment, the Russians launched an offensive on the city. However, the brave defendants of Irevan under Hasan Khan met the advancing Russians with fierce fire at the gates. The Russians lost an enormous number of men and were forced to fall back. The first Russian attack was thus repulsed. The enemy recouped after the losses and undertook another onslaught preceded by destructive artillery fire that practically destroyed the city and set off a huge fire. The southeastern part of the city was occupied. Despite the courageous efforts of Hasan Khan to regroup the defending force, the city was occupied on October 20, 1826.

The Treaty of Turkmenchay

After the occupation of Irevan and Nakhichevan, there was no hurdle left on the way of the Russians and they seized Tabriz and moved towards Tehran. Only the ongoing war with the Ottomans forced the Russians to conclude peace with the Iranians. On February 10, 1828, a peace treaty was signed in the village called Turkmenchay. Under the terms of this agreement, Iran recognized the annexation of Irevan and Nakhichevan to Russia and was deprived of the right to keep a fleet in the Caspian Sea. Iran was also obliged to pay twenty million manats in war reparations to Russia.

This way, Russia occupied the last two Azerbaijani Khanates and there was no rebellion or any other major disturbance until 1916. The Russian rule lasted for 93 years.

The Situation in Iran. Iran sided with Azerbaijan in the wars against Russia and lost many of its sons for the independence of Azerbaijan. That is why I decided to provide the following information about Iran.

The Azerbaijani Issue. As we have already recounted earlier in this book Azerbaijan was divided into two parts: Caucasian and Iranian. The southern part of Azerbaijan remained under Iranian rule. The Khanates of Caucasian Azerbaijan were either fully independent or semi independent. However, Iran, despite the lack of its control over the northern Khanates, still considered them its possessions. No wonder that when Russia attacked Ganja Iran interpreted it as an act of aggression against Iran and started assisting the Azerbaijanis in their resistance wars against Russia.

The War Preparations. Immediately after the occupation of Ganja Iran began the war preparations. In order to reinforce the Azerbaijanis Iran financed the restoration works on many fortresses in Ardebil, Khoy, Tabriz, Nakhichevan, Irevan, Alinjig, and Serdarabad. A Frenchman Monsieur Lamin was invited to do the repair and fortification works exclusively for this purpose. Iran did not have a regular army at that time.

The Iranian army's core consisted of the volunteers from the Azerbaijani-Turkic tribes such as the Shahseven, Afshar, Qajar, Izzaeddinli, Qaragozler and others. Some foreigners were also recruited to the army. A military organization called "Nizami-jedid" was set up. The English officers Mr. Crest and Mr. Lazi who were experts in artillery and infantry were hired to train the Iranian armed forces. There was also an organization of the former soldiers of the Russian army known as "Bahadiran". Prince Abbas

Mirze was appointed the commander in chief of the newly established Iranian armed forces.

A Call for a Holy War. Iran did its best to help Azerbaijan during the Russian invasion. In 1812, the clergy in the holy city of Nejef declared Jihad, that is a holy war against the aggressors. Such prominent religious figures as Sheikh Jafar Nejefi, Mirze Abulgasim Chapligi, Agha Said Ali and others announced that this holy war against the invaders was in full compliance with the Sharia laws.

The Causes of the Defeat. Iran was not prepared for the hostilities properly. The Iranians finished the repair and fortification works in 1809 although the war had started in 1802. They also began creating a regular army in 1809. The holy war was declared only in 1812. The process of army-building was too slow, and many favorable opportunities were missed. The war was waged primarily by the Turkic tribes who were poorly coordinated among themselves.

Iran also lacked the military technology that the enemy had. The Russians had complete superiority over Iran in artillery as well as other branches of the army. Due to these reasons, Iran suffered a defeat at the hands of the Russians. Obviously, the Azerbaijani Khanates were not equipped any better than Iranians. The ultimate outcome of these events was the occupation of Azerbaijan by Russia.

The Situation of Azerbaijan under the Russian Oppression

Azerbaijan could regain its independence only because of the great chaos in the Russian Empire. Let us take a look at the conditions Azerbaijan was under the Russian rule since that will help us understand the main factors that contributed to the collapse of the empire: the Russian oppression and persecution.

The Russification Policies

The Czarist Russia spared no effort to eliminate Turkic national consciousness in Azerbaijan. In other words, they attempted to create a third nation that would eradicate any knowledge of their ties with Turkey or Iran. The Azerbaijani masses were deprived of education and the knowledge of their own history and were made to believe that they were Tartars. The Russians banned any Turkic-language education and never opened a single Turkic language school. The oppressors even wanted to prohibit speaking the native tongue. They constantly forced the population in Azerbaijan to speak Russian only. In the areas where people knew no word of Russian, interpreters were sent, and residents would be still made to speak Russian. There are no words that could describe the kind of injustice and crimes these so-called interpreters perpetrated against naïve Azerbaijani villagers. In an attempt to make Christians the majority in Azerbaijan so that the people in Azerbaijan lose religious ties with Turkey and Iran the Russians were moving Armenians[49], Germans and others from central Russia to Azerbaijan. The Russian authorities even established a special immigration taskforce to implement this wicked plan. Such Christian villages as "Handorf", "Malagan", "Slovakia" and others were created in Ganja. Mughan also witnessed burgeoning Christian settlements. These efforts were directed at Russifying Azerbaijan and increasing the number of Christians in the country.

The Arms Ban

Russia did not draft the Muslims into the army, and the Muslims were deprived of any military training. Instead of military service, the Muslim masses were under heavy army taxation policy. In sharp contrast to the Azerbaijanis, our neighbors were actively recruited and trained in the Russian army. It was not surprising that when the Caucasian countries declared their independence, they had organized armed forces while Azerbaijan had no troops whatsoever. The Russian oppression left us behind in the military area too.

During World War I the Russians tried to make use of the Azerbaijanis as laborers off the front lines. The Azerbaijanis protested saying that "...we are used to weapons, not shovels." The Azerbaijanis were refused such a "privilege" and returned to their homeland. Thus, the Azerbaijanis were stripped of weapons, and there were even attempts to ban a dagger which was part of the national attire.

Obstacles to Education

Until recently there was neither publishing business nor media in Azerbaijan. The publication of Turkic-language newspapers was prohibited. Imagine that ancient Azerbaijan did not have one single

---

[49] Between 1828-1830, over 200,000 Armenians from Iran and Turkey were moved to Azerbaijan while over 100,000 Azerbaijanis were expelled to Iran. By 1886 the number of Armenian settlers on the Azerbaijani lands reached 900,000. In 1828, the Azerbaijanis accounted for 75% of Irevan's population. By 1832, as a result of the mass resettlements Armenians were almost half of the city's population (The publisher's note).

newspaper until very recent times. Although the Russians allowed some education in Azerbaijani Turkish during the last period of the empire, the schools were under strict supervision. For example, the teaching of the Turkic language, geography, history, and other subjects were not permitted. These disciplines could be taught only in Russian. The teachers had to be the citizens of Russia, and the foreign teachers especially from Turkey and Egypt were banned from teaching in Azerbaijani schools. It was almost impossible for the Azerbaijanis to get accepted into Russian secondary schools. Only the wealthy Azerbaijanis could break through racist policies thanks to their money. Below are the statistical data on the number of Muslim-Turkic children in the schools in the Caucasus in 1911:

	Muslim Turks	Georgians	Armenians
Primary Schools	1672	3562	3162
Secondary Schools	796	2650	3861

I hope these figures will give you a clear picture of the situation of the Azerbaijanis in the field of education. Despite the absolute majority of the Muslims in the Caucasus, the number of Muslim children attending schools was the smallest of all. Even those did gain acceptance with incredible difficulties. The higher educational institutions were also closed for the Azerbaijanis. For every thousand Christians only one Turk or Muslim was accepted.

Discrimination in Economic Life

The Russians took drastic measures in order to prevent the Azerbaijanis from acquiring influential positions in the business. The Azerbaijanis were not allowed to own any cotton-producing factories in Mughan. Only Russians and other Christians did have a right to do so. In order not to allow the creation of a Muslim majority anywhere the Russian authorities denied the Caucasians to buy property in Turkestan (Central Asia) and vice versa. The Azerbaijanis were also kept out of the oil business in their own country. So, the Russians deprived the Azerbaijanis of all: education, military service, and economic opportunities.

The Persecution of the Intelligentsia

The nation's intellectuals who had gained education with immense difficulties were under strict control of the authorities[50]. The number of Muslim deputies in the Russian Duma was limited and did not reflect the total number of Muslims in Russia by any means. The Muslims did not have a party of their own and consequently could not have a say in Duma as they wished. Our religious affairs were in the hands of a group of uneducated and obscurantist Iranian-educated mullahs. This situation completely satisfied the Russian authorities while they rejected the graduates of reputed religious institutions.

The Russians were especially active in inciting sectarian conflicts in Azerbaijan. The discord between Sunnis and Shiites was wholeheartedly encouraged. Thus, the Russians appointed a Mufti to be the chief of Sunnis and a Sheykhulislam as the head of Shiites. In order to deepen that religious schism, the Russians opened two religious schools: one called "Omeri" and the other "Alevi". The material situation of the mosques was appalling as well. If before the mosques had been allowed to open small schools with their own funds, now they were deprived even of that right. The religious and national sentiments of the Azerbaijanis had been insulted by the Russians for years.

The Armenian-Azerbaijani Clashes

In 1905, after Russia suffered a defeat in the war with the Japanese, the country began descending into chaos. Workers and peasants were in revolt clashing almost daily with the army and security forces.

In the Caucasus, the Armenians rose up and seized control of their own churches from the Russians. The Armenian Dashnak party which was backed by the Russians against the Ottomans declared their intention to break away from Russia and create an independent state.

The Menshevik party of Russia gained significant support among the people. In the Caucasus, the Georgian nationalists joined this organization. Only the Azerbaijanis were politically passive and still supported the Czarist regime. The Russian secret services took advantage of this situation and dispatched one hundred and thirty secret agents to organize intercommunal violence between the Armenians and

---

[50] A number of our intellectuals have recently been assassinated. Fetheli khan Khoyski, a former foreign minister of Azerbaijan, and Dr. Hasan bey, a former speaker of the Parliament, were murdered in Tiflis. Mr. Behbud Khan Javanshir, a former Interior Minister, was assassinated in Istanbul. They were all assassinated by Armenian terrorists.

Azerbaijanis, the two nations that had lived together for centuries. The clashes began in Baku in 1905, then the violence spread to other parts of the Caucasus. Only these two nations did fight each other while others watched the conflict from the sidelines. The Russians were supplying weapons to both sides in order to inflame the violence further. The violence that started in Baku on February 6th lasted three days. On October 18th of the same year, the Armenians and Azerbaijanis clashed in Ganja. On July 18th of the following year, the bloody incidents happened in Irevan, Qazakh, Karabakh and other areas. The ill-fated Azerbaijanis had no military experience or training for the reasons explained earlier, while the Armenian Dashnaks had been preparing for these kinds of possible conflicts for fifty years both militarily and financially.

Despite those factors, the Azerbaijanis won in the end defeating the Armenians everywhere. However, neither the Azerbaijanis nor Armenians needed this bloodbath. Only the Russians did benefit from these interethnic wars weakening both sides and regaining its influence in the Caucasus. However, these clashes helped the Azerbaijanis to wake up to the realities of the world and get to know their friends and foes. They could finally clearly see and understand the Russian colonial policy towards them.

The Azerbaijanis realized the importance of education and active political life. New schools were opened; societies were set up; newspapers were established[51]. Theater, music and other arts made a stride in the Azerbaijani society. However, the gap between the Azerbaijanis and Armenians remained. In 1914 the Russian government took measures not to allow the Armenian skirmishes in the Caucasus as they would not serve Russian interests at the time. This method of divide and rule was a typical colonial policy of the oppressive Czarist regime.

The Road to Freedom

Our Armenian neighbors obtained the support of America, and the Georgians got the solidarity of the Socialists in Amsterdam in their drive to independence. Only the voice of the downtrodden Azerbaijanis did fall on deaf ears throughout the world. Some Azerbaijanis decided to migrate to Turkey. And despite the Russian efforts to prevent the move some families from Sheki and other cities managed to leave Azerbaijan for

---

[51] Although the first Azerbaijani-language newspaper was published by Hasanbey Zerdabi in 1870, it was very short-lived. The main founders of the modern media publications in Azerbaijan were Mr. Ahmed bey Aghaoghlu and Mr. Alibey Husseynzade.

Turkey. Finally, after the defeat of Russia in the First World War an Armageddonic wind of upheavals began in Russia. The Czarist government was toppled, and Azerbaijan as well as other nations started to feel the breeze of liberation.

"Yes, the oppression has armor and a bullet,
But justice has a proudly held head."

PART SEVEN

The Period of Independent Republic

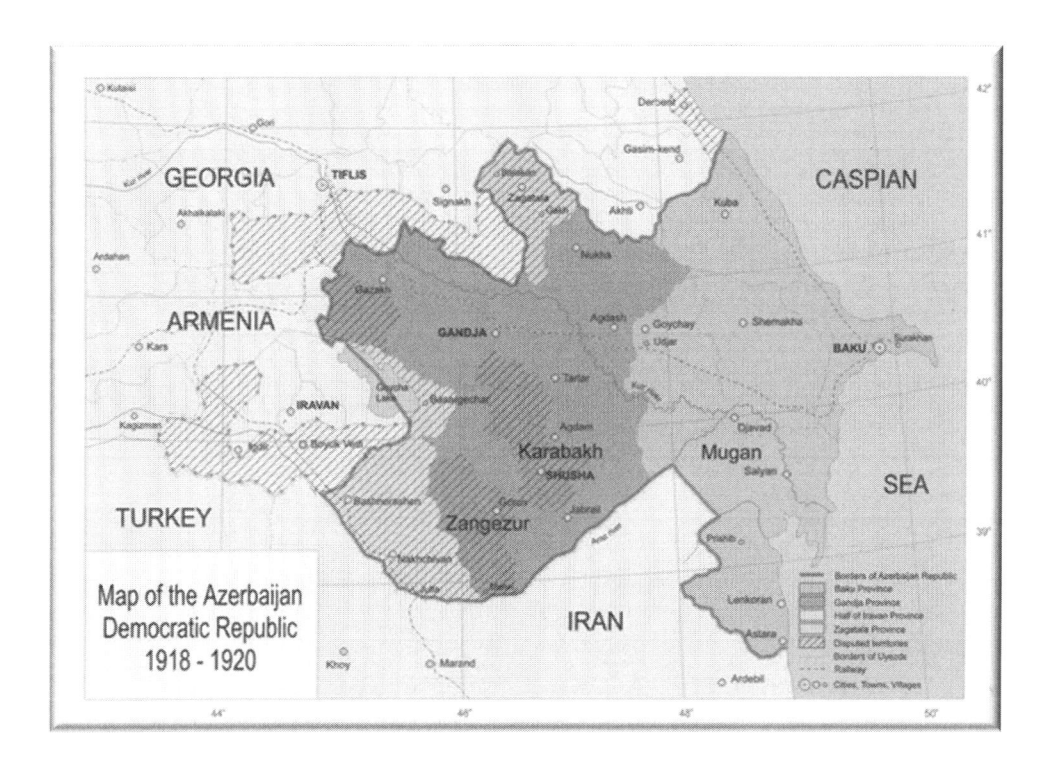

Map of the Azerbaijan Democratic Republic 1918 - 1920

The Great Chaos in Russia

Political events in Russia soon turned into a civil war. Small oppressed nations took advantage of such a situation to secede from Russia and declare their independence. The Russian politicians decided to form some sort of government and parliament. The preparations for the elections were underway when another uprising put the Bolsheviks in charge of Russia. The representatives from the Caucasus who were elected to the Russian parliament decided to set up their regional parliament called "Seym" in Tiflis in order to discuss how to further govern the South Caucasus.

The Seym

On February 25, 1918, the Seym commenced its work. The Armenians were represented by the Dashnak party, the Georgians by the Mensheviks, and the Azerbaijanis by different political parties such as Musavat, Ittihad, Hummet, and others. The class struggle that was waging across Russia took a form of ethnic tensions in the Caucasus. Thus, the Seym became a forum for the expression of the national aspirations of the Caucasians. The Azerbaijanis united into a bloc known as "the Muslim Faction". Unfortunately, not all of the representatives from Azerbaijan could participate in the Seym. Several national political figures were arrested by the enemy who controlled Baku[52]. As the National Committee which was running all the Azerbaijani affairs in Baku was dissolved and its members arrested all the Azerbaijani Turks looked to the Muslim Faction in Tiflis which was their only hope.

The Muslim Faction now had to address many national and social issues in addition to the legal and governmental matters that it originally intended to manage. This bloc of the Azerbaijani parties made sure that the poorly disciplined Russian soldiers who were returning from the WWI fronts went home to Russia via Azerbaijan without causing any incidents. At this time, however, the Armenian Dashnaks were massacring the Turkish and Azerbaijani residents of Kars, Irevan, and looting their possessions. The Armenians were also threatening the Turkish people in Erdehan, Akhsikhe, Borchali, and other cities. The Armenian Dashnaks committed an atrocious bloodbath now known as the infamous March Events in the Azerbaijani capital Baku. During those events, the Armenians annihilated most

---

[52] The allied forces of the Russian Bolsheviks and Armenian Dashnaks seized the power in Baku and perpetrated massacres of Azerbaijani civilians in 1918 (The publisher's note).

Azerbaijanis in and occupied the north-eastern part of Azerbaijan. There was no other organization but the Muslim Faction that could stop the genocide of the Azerbaijanis. But the efforts by the Faction were impeded by the obstacles erected by the so-called Caucasian government who created three armies: Georgian, Armenian, and Azerbaijani. The former two were armed, equipped, and trained while the Azerbaijani armed groups were not given any consideration. To crown it all, the Caucasian government which was set up at the initiative of the Georgians did not send any help to the oppressed people of Baku when they were slaughtered by the Armenian Dashnaks.

The March Tragedy

Approximately thirty or forty thousand Armenian soldiers who demobilized from the Russian army on the German and Austrian fronts arrived in Baku to continue to their homes.

However, their plans were disrupted due to a transport strike, and they stayed in Baku. The Armenian Dashnak party rushed to take advantage of these troops. The Armenian Dashnak propaganda alleged that the Azerbaijanis had begun trouble in order to prevent the soldiers from going to fight the Ottomans. The hungry and embittered Armenian soldiers decided to revenge the residents of Baku. Thus, the Armenian Dashnaks took control of these groups and organized a systematic massacre of the Azerbaijanis in their own capital. This slaughterhouse was portrayed as a Bolshevik-Musavat struggle; the property of the killed was looted. The massacre that started on March 31, 1918, lasted three days. A beautiful national historical building called "Ismailiyye" was burned down. The Armenians shelled and burned the New Pir and other mosques. The number of Azerbaijani civilians killed during this genocide was estimated to reach 15,000 people. The Azerbaijanis who were fortunate to survive escaped to the suburbs of Baku.

Ismailiyye Building burnt by Armenian Dashnaks in Baku, March 1918 (The Academy of Sciences of Azerbaijan is currently located in this building)

These victims were the first heroes to fall for the freedom of Azerbaijan. The Armenian brigands attacked other cities in north-eastern Azerbaijan. They destroyed the city of Shemakha and annihilated its entire population. The Armenians occupied Lenkoran, Salyan, Quba, Hajigabul and Kurdernir and were closing in on Ganja. These ghastly massacres threw the Faction into disarray.

The Armenian Dashnaks made use of the Bolsheviks in this crime as well as Bicherakhov, CentroCaspi and other anti-Turkic groups.

The Azerbaijani army. The Caucasian government in Tiflis created a small armed group of Azerbaijanis to stop further killings in Azerbaijan. The group was sent to Kurdemir to face the outnumbering enemy. The group consisted of the First Tartar (Azerbaijani) regiment, the Second Azerbaijani regiment that was just set up, a Georgian infantry battalion[53] and the Ganja artillery battery. Altogether they were only one thousand fighters. Five thousand Bashipozugs expressed their willingness to fight the Armenian gangs but were refused for their pillaging in previous battles. Only this small group did stand up to the enemy. The regiments took up a position near Yevlakh and were to secure and defend the famous major bridge over the Kura River. The onslaughts of the Armenians could not break through the heroic defense of these fighters. The newly born Azerbaijani army held the enemy at that position until the Ottoman army arrived and performed its brotherly duty. That fledgling Azerbaijani force fought bravely against the enemy shoulder to shoulder with the Ottoman army all the way until Baku was liberated.

---

[53] The Georgian battalion was sent to help the Azerbaijanis to liberate Baku from the Armenian Dashnaks. The Georgians returned to their country after the arrival of the Turkish army.

The Massacres

The Armenian Dashnaks who turned the east of Azerbaijan into a scene of carnage continued with their atrocities in the south of the country too. The Azerbaijani population of the Irevan region was entirely annihilated, and the towns and villages were demolished by the Armenian generals Andranik, Dro and others. The Azerbaijani refugees from that massacre flooded into Ganja. The events in Irevan caused a big scandal in the Seym. The actions of the Armenian brigands were discussed very emotionally at the sessions on February 5, 7, 19, and 20. A special delegation was dispatched to Irevan. This fact finding delegation returned after having investigated the facts of the massacres. The group proved that 211 Azerbaijani villages were destroyed, and one hundred thousand people were murdered by the Armenians. The Seym allocated 15 million rubles to assist the refugees, but actually disbursed only 3 million. This meager amount did not meet the needs of the poor, tortured and downtrodden Azerbaijani refugees. Hence, there were only three thousand Azerbaijanis left in Irevan out of three hundred thousand under the Czar.

The situation in the Caucasus was out of control. The domestic and foreign affairs were deteriorating with every hour. The Caucasian government decided to send a special peace delegation to Turkey to sign a peace accord. However, the Turks did not recognize that group. The independence of the region was necessary to make the peace efforts legitimate. Finally, after extremely fiery discussions the independence of the Caucasus was declared at the session of the Seym on April 19th.

The All-Caucasian Republic

The independence was declared, and the delegation was sent to Trabzon for peace negotiations with Turkey again. However, the talks dragged on. The Ottomans demanded Kars, Erdehan and Batum after the Brest-Litovsk agreement. The Georgians and Armenians did not accept those demands and had to return home empty-handed. Right after this failure, the Ottoman army resumed its offensive.

Naturally, the Azerbaijanis were not in agreement with their neighbors regarding this matter and kept inviting them to discuss the issues with the Ottoman government peacefully. At this time numerous popular delegations from Azerbaijan and Daghestan traveled to Trabzon, Batum and Istanbul demanding unity with Turkey. After these events, even the Azerbaijani members of the Seym were under the shadow of a doubt by others. Finally, the Azerbaijani deputies left the Seym in protest to the resumed hostilities in the southern Caucasus.

The head of the negotiating team that arrived in Trabzon was Chekhingili, a Georgian national, who sincerely desired peace in the Caucasus. He left the team in Trabzon and returned to Tiflis to lobby for the peace effort. Meanwhile, Enver Pasha arrived in Trabzon. The team was preparing for the talks. After the defeat of the Georgian and Armenian units on the Ottoman front and due to indefatigable peace efforts of Chekhingili, the Georgians joined the Azerbaijanis in their drive for peace with the Ottomans. The Caucasian government sent a new peace team this time to Batum which was taken by the Ottomans. But the negotiations collapsed again. This time the stumbling block was the city of Batum that the Georgians claimed as their own. The position of the Ottomans on this issue was also known to the participants. Enver Pasha told the Georgians at one of the meetings:" Your claim to Batum is irrelevant as revolutionary Russia has conceded that Batum is an ancient Turkish city. That is why I would advise you not to follow the example of the Dashnaks, and I will readily recognize the independence of Georgia."

The Triumvirate in the Caucasus

The differences among the Azerbaijanis, Georgians, and Armenians because of the Ottoman question remained. The Azerbaijanis left the Seym when the Georgians and Armenians went to war with the Ottomans. That is why a new three-man government was set up, and in order to keep the Azerbaijanis out of this government, the Seym was dissolved. The relations deteriorated even more after the **grave** situation in Baku. When the Armenian Dashnaks killed, burned, and looted in eastern Azerbaijan from Baku to Kurdemir the Georgians and Armenians in the government looked the other way. They did not even attempt to intervene to stop the massacres of the Azerbaijani civilians. The Armenian Dashnaks whose representatives were also members of the Seym joined the Bolsheviks in Baku and protested the work of the Seym. The Georgians who did not voice any protest against the inferno in Azerbaijan took drastic measures to nip any Bolshevik activity in the bud in their own country. The only demonstration organized by the Bolsheviks in the Alexandrov Garden in Tiflis was dispersed using gunfire. Such was the position of our neighbors regarding the massacres of the Azerbaijani civilians by the Armenian Dashnaks in Baku.

The Azerbaijani armed groups that were set up by the Seym for formality were not equipped even with light arms. Our troops had to use the weapons that were taken by the Azerbaijani villagers from the Russian troops. The Muslim Faction could not tolerate such a situation and gave an ultimatum to the Seym and the peace negotiating team in Batum that " ...if such a situation continues the Azerbaijanis will resign from the Seym and declare the independence of Azerbaijan."

About Baku

Baku is the capital of the Republic of Azerbaijan. Before the emergence of Baku, a little village of Surakhani to the west of the city used to be a famous place throughout the region and beyond. An ancient fire-worshipping temple located there earned Surakhani such fame. Zoroastrian pilgrims from all over the East especially India had flocked to this small village. It is believed that at this period in our history Indian pilgrims founded the city of Baku which means " towards the truth" in Hindi (Gujarat). All the available materials reinforce that supposition. Therefore, it is senseless to search for the meaning of Baku in Persian. Baku was mentioned the first time in the written history in the tenth century by Mesudi as " Bakube".

The Nobel Brothers' Oil Derricks in Baku, early 20th Century

Baku used to be a tiny village in Shirvan. Later in history Baku seceded from Shirvan and became an independent Khanate, thus transforming into a mid-sized city. Until the Russian occupation (1806) and for about fifty years (1872) after that Baku preserved the status of a medium-sized city. However, after 1872 a breakneck boom began in Baku due to its vast oil and gas resources. In a very short time, Baku became a large and wealthy city. The population of Baku reached 400,000 in 1917. There were forty thousand workers in the oil fields half of which were Turkic and Muslim. The oil was extracted in Baku from ancient times utilizing the manual labor and barrels for overseas exports. Under the Russians, these primitive methods were still used from 1806 to 1872. The amount of oil extracted through this method in Baku reached: 2,800 tons in 1850 and 80,000 tons in 1872.

Finally, thanks to foreign oil investors the Baku oil industry went through rapid modernization by introducing a drilling system used in the oilfields of the United States of America. The first boring well was used in 1872. Shortly thereafter, all manual extraction methods were gone. The following are the number of wells and oil production volumes extracted using the new technology: The Year 1879: 250 wells, 480K tons; 1900: 2,800 wells, 7,526,000 tons; 1905: 3,700 wells, 10,400,000 tons.

Soon the Baku oil was competing with the energy resources from the rest of the world. In a short period, the Azerbaijani oil industry drove its American competitors out of the entire Russian market and its oil was now exported to Asia and Europe. The oilfields are located outside Baku in the suburbs of Bibiheybet (five kilometers to the south of Baku), Balakhani, Sabunchu, Surakhani, Binegedi, etc. which are approximately 25 to 30 kilometers to the northeast of the capital city. The oil is delivered to the refineries in Baku via oil pipelines. Different petroleum products such as petrol gas, automobile petrol/gasoline, Vaseline, Paraffin wax, and others are produced in Baku refineries and exported overseas.

Oil is also transported by air and water. The pipeline stretching from Baku to Batum carries almost 400,000 tons of oil to other countries annually. If the government collected only ten kopeks on every pood (sixteen kilos) in oil taxes the revenue from the oil alone would reach *50* or 60 million gold rubles. Baku is also rich with fish and sturgeon caviar. The resources mentioned above in addition to available ships and planes earned Baku the name of "the prolific gold sea". So, this is Baku, the city that attracts both aggressors and admirers.

The End of the All-Caucasian Government

One of the Azerbaijani members had spoken at one of the meetings of the Seym before the negotiations in Batum took place. He announced that in order to save Azerbaijan from the Armenian gangs and political chaos Azerbaijan needed outside help. He went into great length expounding on the immediate need for that assistance, and that the only power that could rescue Azerbaijan was our brethren from Turkey. The Seym member emphasized that the Azerbaijani faction fully realized that our neighbors would not endorse this move, but the urgency of the matter dictated that the Ottomans be invited to Azerbaijan at once.

Although, a group of the Caucasian negotiators had already left for Batum for a meeting with the Ottomans because of the major differences among the three constituent factions of the Seym the Caucasian government was heading towards collapse. On March 25, 1918, the

Azerbaijani faction held its emergency meeting in one of the Tiflis palaces. It was announced that the Georgians were planning to break away from the Seym and declare their independence. The Azerbaijanis were warned to get ready for possible complications resulting from the disintegration of the Seym. That meeting ended with no specific results. Another special meeting was convened the same night this time with the participation of the Georgian leaders: Messrs. Chkheidze, Sereteli and Kinchikhuri.

The head of the Azerbaijani faction introduced Sereteli who stated: " I am authorized by the Menshevik party and the Georgian faction of the Seym to announce that we failed to hold a session of the factions from the three nations. That is why our faction declared the independence of Georgia. We hope that in the future we will succeed in creating a union that was impossible today."

Then Chkheidze expressed his regret about the dissolution of the Caucasian union. Late Fetheli Khan Khoyski, the head of the Azerbaijani faction, responded with the following words:" I consider the separation of these three Caucasian nations very unlikely since these nations are tied to one another in many intricate ways. However, if the Georgians declare the independence of their country, the Azerbaijanis will carry out their duties accordingly!"

The Georgians left the session. The Armenians had similar plans. The meeting concluded with the idea that "if Georgia wants independence, Azerbaijan should declare its independence immediately".

The following day the last and historic session of the Seym was held. The Georgians tried to blame the Azerbaijanis for the dissolution of the union, but after strong speeches from the Azerbaijani members that refuted those allegations, the Georgians stopped their accusations. After long mutual diatribes, the parliamentarians adopted the following resolution and lowered the curtain on the Seym stage for the last time.

"Due to the differences among the nations regarding war and peace and the inability of the Caucasian government to become a strong and influential political power this meeting of the Seym declares the Seym defunct and dissolved." This session took place on May 26, 1918.

Thus, the Caucasian government and its Seym was dissolved, and three new republics: Azerbaijan, Georgia and Armenia were born. Meanwhile, Nuru Pasha and Nayim bey arrived in Ganja with several other officers of the Turkish army to placate the nervous Azerbaijanis. The Azerbaijani faction's provisional "the Azerbaijani National Council" ceased its activities in Tiflis.

The Cabinet of Ministers of Azerbaijan, 1919

The Republic of Azerbaijan
The Declaration of Independence

On May 28, 1918, the National Council declared the independence of Azerbaijan and instructed late Fetheli Khan to form the first national cabinet of ministers.

The First Government of Independent Republic of Azerbaijan

The National Council approved the first government. Here are some important ministries and their heads:

Fetheli Khan Khoyski - The Speaker of the parliament and Justice Minister
Behbud bey Javanshir - Minister of Internal Affairs
Mohammed Hasan bey - Minister of Foreign Affairs
Nesib bey Yusifbeyli - Minister of Education
Khudadat bey - Minister of Transportation

Other ministers included Khudadat bey Refibeyli, Alimerdan bey Topchibashli and others. There were twelve ministries altogether. The National Council moved from Tiflis to Ganja since Baku was under the Armenian-Bolshevik occupation. The government sent notes to neighboring countries and governments of European and American nations informing them of the newly independent country.

The Liberation of Baku

The Turkish armed forces invited by the Azerbaijani National Council arrived in Azerbaijan via Gyumri and Aghstafa and joined the Azerbaijani troops in Kurdemir and Hajigabul in Central Azerbaijan. Although the military advance was impeded by some political considerations the joint Azerbaijani-Turkish forces reached Baku and liberated the capital from the Armenian-Bolshevik cutthroats on September 14, 1918. Other parts of Azerbaijan were also freed from the aggressors. The government of Azerbaijan moved from Ganja to Baku.

The Turkish-Azerbaijani army marching in Baku after the liberation from the Armenian Dashnaks and Bolsheviks (Sept 2018)

The Recognition of Independence

The government of the young Azerbaijani Republic did an arduous work for two years dispatching delegations to Europe in order to gain international recognition. At last, on January 12, 1920, the countries of the Entente: England, France, and Italy officially recognized the Azerbaijani Republic. The same year Azerbaijan signed numerous political and economic treaties with the neighboring countries including Iran.

The Bibliography

Besides the events and stories from my extensive travel throughout Azerbaijan, I have also used the following books and publications when I was working on this book.

1. Tarikhi govmu Turk (history of the Turks) by Hasan Ata
2. Shejereyi-Turkiye by Emir Gazi Bahadur Khan
3. The Turkish History by Hejib Asim
4. The Ottoman History by Ahmed Rasim
5. Gamus ul Alam by Shemseddin Sami bey
6. Rovzat ul sefa by Emir Khudavend shah
7. Habib us siyar by Khandemir
8. Nuzhet ul Gulub by Hamdullah Mustovfi
9. Tarikhi Gozide by Hamdullah Mustovfi
10. The History by Molla Esher
11. Muesser Sultani by Abdulrazzag Dunbullu
12. Mirat ul Buldani by Nasiri
13. The History by Teberi
14. Azerbaijani Fireworshipping Temples by Lutfeli bey Azer
15. The Muslim Dynasties by Lan Paul
16. The Museum of Dar happiness by Humayun Publishers
17. The coins of the Jelairids by Markov
18. Caspian by Dori
19. The Occupied Caucasus by Kaspari
20. The Ancient History of the Caucasus by Shopen

I have also made extensive use of daily Azerbaijani and Russian publications, the Russian geographical magazines, the works of the Caucasian Archeological Society, the official calendar of the Caucasus of 1917, and other materials.

CHRONOLOGY OF KEY EVENTS IN AZERBAIJAN'S HISTORY

1.2 m - 1 m years BCE – The Azikh Cave civilization (Western Azerbaijan)

6-4 Centuries BCE – The Shomu Tepe Culture (Western Azerbaijan)

4-3 Centuries BCE – The Kura-Arax Culture, Early Bronze era, (Central Azerbaijan)

The first half of the 9th Century BCE - The kingdom of Manna

670's BCE - The kingdom of Midia (Southern Azerbaijan)

The 4th Century BCE - The state of Atropatena with Atropat as the first ruler (Southern Azerbaijan)

The 4th Century BCE - The kingdom of Albania (known as Caucasian Albania versus Albania in the Balkans)

80-90 - The Roman military incursion into Albania

313 - Adoption of Christianity as the state religion in Albania

The 5th Century - Creation of the Albanian alphabet

The first half of the 6th Century - New incursions of the Turkic tribes into South Caucasus including the Sabirs, Avars, Bulgars and Khazars

626 - Large-scale migration of the Turkic Khazars into Albania

629-630 - Conquest of Albania by the Turkic Khazars

639-640 – The first failed attempts to invade Azerbaijan by the Arab armies. Javanshir rules Albania

643 – The Arab armies invade Azerbaijan. The Battle of Ardebil, the Battle of Derbend (Bab Al Abvab)

644 - Mugan (Azerbaijan) and Tiflis (Tbilisi, Georgia) are conquered by the Arabs

644 – The first defeat of the Arabs at Belenjer

652-653 – The Arab armies under Salman Ibn Rabiya attack Derbend. Salman is killed in a Khazar-Arab clash near Belenjer. Most of Azerbaijan is liberated from the Arab armies

654-655 – The Arab armies capture northern part of Azerbaijan

654 - Javanshir signs an agreement with Konstantin II of Byzantium

664 - Javanshir signs a peace accord with the Khazars, he marries a daughter of the Khazar Khagan

670 - Javanshir meets with the Arab Calif Al Muaviyya who appoints Javanshir the ruler of Albania

680 - Javanshir is killed in a plot by his own nobles

680 - New Khazar incursions

Late 7th- early 8th Centuries - Moisey Kalankatuyski writes "The History of Albanians"

705 – The Albanian state is abolished. A new province called Arran is established under the Arab rule

The 8th Century - The Sufi movement begins

707-708 – The Arab-Khazar wars in Azerbaijan

721-722 - More Turkic tribes enter Azerbaijan including the Khazars, Kipchaks and others

748-752 – An anti-Arab uprising in Azerbaijan

763-764 - A new Khazar raid into Arran and Iberia (Georgia)

808-809 - An uprising by the Khurramdin Movement against the Arab rule in Azerbaijan and some cities in Iran

816 - Babek becomes the leader of the Khurramdin Uprising

830-833 - Babek's forces seize Hamadan

836 - The death of Tarkhan, one of Babek's generals, an ethnic Turk

837 – The Arabs take Babek's castle. Babek is executed the following year

Late 9th-early 10th Centuries – The Arab grip on Azerbaijan weakens, the emergence of new feudal states

1015-1029 TheOghuz Turks enter Azerbaijan

1038– The establishment of an Oghuz Turkic state in Central Asia

1054 - Toghrul, the Sultan of the Oghuz Turks, conquers Tabriz (Southern Azerbaijan)

Late 11th Century – The Oghuz Turkic Sultans Alp Arslan and Melik-Shah conquer the rest of Azerbaijan and neighboring countries

1071 – The Battle of Malazgirt, Alp Arslan routs the Byzantium army

1079– The construction of the Siniq Qala mosque in Baku

1089-1183 - Mehseti Khanim Ganjavi, a prominent Azerbaijani poetess

1157 - The reign of Sultan Sanjar, the last great sultan of the Seljukids

1118 – The Emergence of the Iraq Sultanate of Seljuks with Hamadan as the capital city

1141-1209 - Nizami Ganjavi, one of the greatest Azerbaijani poets

1148– The construction of the Qirmizi Gunbez (Red Dome) mausoleum in Maraga, Southern Azerbaijan

1136-1225 - The Atabeg Eldegiz State of Azerbaijan

1160 - Shamsaddin Eldegiz of Azerbaijan becomes the Great Atabeg of the Seljuks

1161 – The Georgian troops invade the territories of the Azerbaijani Atabegs and sack the cities of Ani, Dvin and Ganja

1163 - Atabeg Shamsaddin Eldegiz liberates Ani and Dvin, and in turn invades Georgia

1175 - The Atabeg State of Azerbaijan takes control of Tabriz

1186-1191 - The reign of Atabeg Qizil Arslan

1187 - The Construction of the Mardakan Fortress near Baku

1188 - Qizil Arslan conquers Hamadan and becomes the Seljuk Sultan

1192 - The transfer of the capital city of Shirvan from Shemakha to Baku

1216– The construction of the Albanian Gandzasar Monastery in Karabakh

1220 - First Mongol campaigns into Azerbaijan

1225 - The end of the Atabeg State of Azerbaijan

1231 - The Mongols occupy Shirvan

1235 - The Mongols enter Ganja

1239 - The fall of Derbend and Mongol occupation of Azerbaijan

1239-1256 - Azerbaijan is governed by a viceroy of the Great Mongol Khan

1256-1357 - The State of Ilkhanids in Azerbaijan

1259 – The construction of the Maraga astronomy observatory

1295-1304 - Gazan Khan's reign. Gazan Khan converts to Islam

1308– The great mathematician Ubeyd Tabrizi

The 14th century – The completion of the construction of the Mardakan, Nardaran, Ramana and Ark fortresses near Baku

The 14the Century – The construction of the Shirvanshah Palace in Baku

1340-1357 - The Chobanid rule in Azerbaijan

1359-1410 - Azerbaijan under the Jelairids

1369-1417 - Imadeddin Nasimi, one of the greatest poets in the history of Azerbaijan, is born in Shemakha, Azerbaijan, died and was buried in Aleppo, Syria

1386-1399 – The military campaigns of Tamerlane into Azerbaijan. Tamerlane's attempts to seize the Alinjaqala fortress

1410-1467 - The Qaraqoyunlu State of Azerbaijan

1410-1420 - The reign of Qara Yusif Qaraqoyunlu

1435-1467 - The reign of Jahanshah Qaraqoyunlu

1453-1457 - Jahanshah subjugates Iran

1453-1478 - The rule of Uzun Hasan Aghqoyunlu

1465 – The construction of the Blue Mosque in Tabriz

1472-1473 – The Aghqoyunlu-Ottoman wars

1487 - Ismail Safavid, the future Shah Ismail and the founder of the Safavid dynasty, is born in Ardebil

1494-1556 - Mohammed Fizuli, one of the greatest poets in the Azerbaijani history

1500 - Ismail Safavid arrives in Erzinjan

1501 - Ismail takes Baku; Ismail routs Elvend Aghqoyunlu's troops in Sharur

1501 - Ismail ascends to the throne in Tabriz and is declared the Shah. The establishment of the Azerbaijani Safavid State

1501-1524 - The reign of Shah Ismail I

1508 - Shah Ismail conquers Baghdad

1514 – The Safavid-Ottoman wars, the Battle of Chaldiran

1521 – The Georgian Principalities become vassal states of the Safavids

1524 - Shah Ismail I's death; Shah Tehmasib I ascends to the Safavid throne

1534-1554 - The military campaigns of the Ottoman Sultan Suleyman to Azerbaijan

1538 - Shirvan becomes part of the Safavid State

1551 - Sheki becomes part of the united Azerbaijani Safavid State

1552 - The Safavid military campaigns into the Ottoman territories

1555 - The Safavids move their capital from Tabriz to Qazvin

1587-1629 - Shah Abbas I as the Safavid ruler

1598 - Shah Abbas I moves the Safavid capital from Qazvin to Isfahan

1603-1607 – The new Safavid-Ottoman wars

1613 - Shah Abbas I's invasion of Georgia

1630 - The Ottoman army captures Irevan from Azerbaijan

1717-1797 - Molla Penah Vagif, a famous Azerbaijani poet in Karabakh

1722 - The first Russian incursion under Peter I

1723 - A Russian flotilla occupies Baku

1726 – The Russians occupy a number of cities on the Caspian coast

1736 - Nadir Shah of the Oghuz Turkic Afshar tribe becomes the ruler of Iran and Azerbaijan. The Afsharids Dynasty rules until 1796. Russian troops eventually withdraw from the Azerbaijani coastal areas

1740's - **Southern Azerbaijan** includes the following Khanates: the Tabriz Khanate, Urmiyye Khanate, Khoy Khanate, Qaradagh Khanate, Serab Khanate, Maragha Khanate, Maku Khanate and Ardebil Khanate

Northern Azerbaijan: the Karabakh Khanate, Sheki Khanate, Quba Khanate, Shemakha Khanate, Irevan Khanate, Nakhichevan Khanate, Talish Khanate, Ganja Khanate, Baku Khanate and Javad Khanate

1748- 1763 - Panahali Khan rules the Karabakh Khanate

1750 - The city of Shusha originally known as Panahabad is founded as the capital of the Karabakh Khanate

1758-1789 - Fath Ali Khan as the ruler of the Quba Khanate in Northern Azerbaijan

1763 – The construction of the Askeran Fortress in Karabakh

1783 - Kartli Kakheti kingdom of Georgia becomes a protectorate of Russia

1783-1814 - Javad Khan's reign as the Khan of Ganja

1795 - The siege of Shusha by Agha Muhammad Shah Qajar

1796-1925 - The reign of the Qajar Dynasty from the Azerbaijani Turkic Qajar tribe over Iran and most of southern Azerbaijan

1797 – The assassination of Agha Mohammed Shah Qajar in Shusha

1803 – The Russian conquest of northern Azerbaijan begins

1804 – The Russo-Iranian wars over Azerbaijan break out

1805 – An agreement between Russia and the Karabakh Khanate; an agreement between Russia and the Shirvan Khanate

1806 – The assassination of the Russian general Tsitsianov near Baku

1806 – The Sheki Khanate pushes Russian troops out; Derbend is taken by the Russians; the Baku and Quba Khanates are conquered by Russia

Late 1806 - A Russo-Ottoman war breaks out

1810 – The Russians seize Megri

1810 – A military pact between the Qajars and the Ottomans against Russia

1813 – The Gulustan Treaty between Russia and the Qajar State whereas the Azerbaijani lands to the north of the Arax river become Russian possessions

1815 - Von Diez, a German translator, translates Kitabi Dede Qorqud, a famous Turkic epic tale about the Oghuz Turkmen tribes living in Azerbaijan and Eastern Anatolia, into German and makes it popular in the West

1826 - Abbas Mirza Qajar, the crown prince of Iran, heads a large-scale offensive against the Russians in northern Azerbaijan

1826 - A full-blown uprising against the Russians in Ganja; The Battle of Ganja

Late 1826 – The Russian troops defeat the Azerbaijani-Iranian forces and begin offensive south of the river Arax

1827 – The Russians take Nakhichevan, Abbasabad, Serdarabad, the Irevan Fortress

Late 1827 - The Russian army occupies Marand, Khoy and Tabriz in southern Azerbaijan

1828 - Urmiyye and Ardebil fall to the Russian troops

1828 – The Treaty of Turkmenchay between Russia and Iran under which all of Northern Azerbaijan's occupation by Russia is finalized

1830 - Jar and Jar-Belokan uprising against Russia

1831 – An anti-Russian uprising in Talysh

1836 - The Russian Tsar abolishes the Albanian Apostolic Church and transfers all its churches and assets to the Armenian church

1837 – An anti-Russian uprising in Quba

1838 - Anti-colonial uprisings in Sheki and Jar-Belokan

1844-45 - Peasant uprisings against Russians in Shusha, Sheki and Quba

1863 – An uprising in Zakatala

1863 - Alimardan bey Topchubashli, a prominent Azerbaijani politician and a speaker of the parliament of independent Azerbaijan, is born in Tiflis. Died in Paris in 1934

1864 - Ali bey Huseynzade, a prominent Azerbaijani political and public figure, is born in Salyan, Azerbaijan. Died in Istanbul in 1940

1869 - Ahmed bey Aghaoghlu, the founder of Difai party of Azerbaijan and one of the most prominent independence leaders in Azerbaijan and later in Turkey, is born in Shusha, Azerbaijan. Died in Istanbul in 1939

1873 - The first oil fountain in Baku

1874 - The first female school opens in Baku

1875 - The first national democratic publication "Ekinchi" is founded

1875 - Fatali Khan Khoyski, the first prime minister of the Azerbaijan Democratic Republic, is born in Sheki, Azerbaijan. Assassinated by an Armenian terrorist in Tiflis in 1920

1884 - Memmed Emin Resulzade, one of the founders of the future Azerbaijan Democratic Republic, is born in Novkhani, near Baku

1898 - Baku surpasses the US in oil production

1901 - Haji Zeynalabdin Taghiev, one of the most prominent oil magnates and philanthropists, founds the first school for Muslim girls

1903 - The first Azerbaijan Turkish language newspaper "Sherqi Rus" is founded in Tiflis

1905 - The establishment of the Turkic Revolutionary Committee of Social Federalists in Ganja

1905 – The Armenian-Azerbaijani Clashes in Baku and other parts of Azerbaijan

1905 - The establishment of the "Geyrat" (Honor) organization in Ganja

1905– The establishment of the "Difai" (Defence) Party in Azerbaijan with the main objective of protecting Azerbaijani civilians from Armenian armed gangs and massacres

1906 - The satirical magazine "Molla Nasreddin" begins publishing in Tiflis

1906 - Mohammad Hossein Shahriyar, a great Azerbaijani poet of the 20th century, is born in Tabriz. Died in Tehran in 1988

1908 - Baku sees the first opera in the Muslim East: "Leyli and Majnun" by Uzeyir bey Hajibeyli, the most famous Azerbaijani composer

1911 – The establishment of the Musavat Party (Equality) that later became the main pro-independence political force in northern Azerbaijan

1911 - The first women's publication "Ishiq" (Light)

1916 - The premiere of the Opera "Shah Ismail" by Muslim Magomayev in Baku

1917 - A political party Turki Adami Merkeziyyet (Turkic Centralist party) is founded in Ganja.

1918 – The Armenian Dashnaks massacre Azerbaijani civilians in and around Ganja

March 1918 – The Bolsheviks and Armenian Dashnaks massacre thousands of Azerbaijani civilians in Baku and other east Azerbaijani cities and towns

27 May 1918 – The Azerbaijani National Council is convened

28 May 1918 – The Azerbaijan Democratic Republic, the first republic in the Turkic and Muslim world, is declared

4 June 1918 - Azerbaijan and Ottoman Turkey sign a peace and friendship agreement

26 June 1918 - The establishment of the National Army of Azerbaijan; The Turkic (Azerbaijani) language is declared the state language of Azerbaijan

31 July 1918 - The collapse of the Baku People's Commissars' (Bolsheviks) in Baku

August 1918 - The arrival of the first English military expeditionary corps to support the Bolsheviks headed by Shaumyan

15 September 1918 – The united Ottoman-Azerbaijani forces liberate Baku from the Bolsheviks and Armenian Dashnaks; The capital is moved from Ganja to Baku

5 October 1918 - the Azerbaijani government privatizes the oil industry after the fall of the Bolshevik regime

9 November 1918 - The new tri-color national flag is adopted which is still used today

7 December 1918 - The first session of the Parliament of the independent Azerbaijani Republic

1919 - Azerbaijan becomes the first Muslim country to introduce universal suffrage thus enfranchising women

1919 - Georgia and Azerbaijan sign a pact of recognition and mutual defense of territorial integrity

1 September 1919 – The Baku University founded by the Parliament

11 January 1920 - The de-facto recognition of Azerbaijan's independence by the Supreme War Council of the Allies at the Paris Peace Conference

20 March 1920 – An Iranian-Azerbaijani agreement is signed; Iran recognizes Azerbaijan's independence

27 April 1920 - The Russian 11th Red Army invades Azerbaijan and occupies Baku; The start of the Soviet occupation of Azerbaijan

24 May 1920 - The Soviets nationalize the oil industry

End of May 1920 - A large-scale uprising against the Soviet power in Ganja.

Early June 1920 - A large-scale uprising against the Soviet occupation in Shusha, Karabakh, an uprising in Zakatala

19 June 1920 - The assassination of Fatali Khan Khoyski, a former Prime Minister, by an Armenian terrorist in Tiflis

28 July 1920 - Nakhichevan is occupied by the Soviet army

20 September 1920 - Mohammed Khiyabani, the head of an anti-English and anti-monarchy movement in Tabriz, Southern Azerbaijan, Iran, is killed after the movement is crushed

13 October 1921 - The Kars Agreement between Turkey on the one hand and Azerbaijan, Armenian and Georgian Soviet Socialist Republics on the other is signed. The document delineates the borders among these countries

1922 - The Central Committee of Azerbaijan Communist Part decrees to change the Azerbaijani Turkic alphabet from Arabic to Latin

1923 - The new alphabet is adopted

1929 - The official transition to the Latin alphabet

1940 - The official transition of the Azerbaijani Turkic alphabet from Latin to Cyrillic

1941-1942 - Azerbaijan sets up a number of Soviet army divisions consisting of mostly ethnic Azerbaijanis: the 402nd, 223rd, 416th, 77th, 271st Azerbaijani divisions

1941 – The Soviet troops enter northern Iran (Southern Azerbaijan) while the allied British troops enter other parts of Iran

1945 – The Azerbaijan People's Government is established in Southern Azerbaijan (Northwestern Iran) with the support from the USSR. Tabriz is the capital of the new state.

1946 - The Shah government crushes the new Azerbaijani state after the withdrawal of the Soviet troops. The Iranian troops brutalize the local population in Tabriz and other Azerbaijani cities

1947 - A Soviet decree to deport 100,000 Azerbaijanis from their ancestral homes in the Armenian SSR to the Azerbaijan SSR

1955 – The death of Memmed Emin Resulzade, one of the founders of Azerbaijani Democratic Republic, in Ankara, Turkey

17 November 1988 - The beginning of the independence movement in the Azerbaijan SSR

1988 – The Armenian authorities expel all Azerbaijanis from their ancestral lands in the Armenian SSR

20 January 1990 - The Soviet troops enter Baku to crush the independence movement. Hundreds of civilians killed, more wounded. The day is commemorated as "Black January" in Azerbaijan

5 February 1991 – The Azerbaijan SSR becomes the Azerbaijan Republic

18 October **1991** - Azerbaijan becomes independent of the Soviet Union

26 February 1992 – The Armenian armed forces perpetrate an act of genocide in the Azerbaijani city of Khojali killing hundreds of unarmed civilians including women and children

1992 - Abulfaz Elchibey becomes the President of the Azerbaijan Republic

1992-1993 - Armenia occupies 20% of Azerbaijan's internationally recognized territory, expels over 800,000 Azerbaijani civilians from their homes in Azerbaijan proper

3 October 1993 - Heydar Aliyev becomes the President of the Azerbaijan Republic

15 October 2003 - Ilham Aliyev becomes the President of the Azerbaijan Republic

2004 – The Azerbaijan Republic opens its consulate in Tabriz, the capital of East Azerbaijan province of Iran

2009 - The Turkic Council is founded in Nakhichevan, Azerbaijan. The Turkic Council members include Azerbaijan, Kazakhstan, Kyrgyzstan, Turkey, and Uzbekistan. Hungary is an observer member

April 2016 – The Azerbaijani Army rolls back an Armenian offensive and liberates strategic areas in the Karabakh region including an important hill called Lala Tepe

Printed in Poland
by Amazon Fulfillment
Poland Sp. z o.o., Wrocław